Easy Peasy
Language Arts 5
Lesson Guide

Welcome to the EP Language Arts 5 Lesson Guide!

This book teaches the lessons you'll need to complete the Language Arts 5 Workbook. This book was made for the student to use. Read the lesson each day and then follow the directions on your worksheet for that day in your workbook.

The answers for the workbook are in the back of this book. Complete your worksheet before checking your answers. Learn from your mistakes. Mistakes are learning opportunities. Don't waste your opportunities! If you cheat and just copy answers, you are only cheating yourself. The point is to learn and to educate yourself. Education is power. Cheating is lazy. Lazy people aren't powerful!

This course covers all language arts topics including: writing, grammar, and spelling. Throughout the year students will be writing non-fiction essays and the year ends with writing a novel. You will practice creative, descriptive writing, including writing with similes, metaphors, alliteration, and onomatopoeia. You will learn and practice the six traits of writing.

If you get to the end of a page, turn the page to see if there is more to your lesson!

Have a great year!

Day 1

1. Read this stanza. (A stanza is a section of a poem. There is a space between each stanza to show you where one stops and the next starts.)
   - I have you fast in my fortress,
     And will not let you depart,
     But put you down into the dungeon
     In the round-tower of my heart.
2. In the stanza what two words rhyme?
3. A rhyme scheme tells you how many lines the stanzas have and which lines of the stanza rhyme. We write a rhyme scheme using letters, and matching letters show which lines rhyme. If it was an AABB rhyme scheme, then the first two lines would rhyme and the third and fourth lines would rhyme.
4. The rhyme scheme in this poem is ABCB. That means that each stanza in this poem has four lines. The matching letters tell you which lines rhyme. In this poem the B lines rhyme, meaning the second and fourth lines rhyme. The A and C lines have no matching letter, so no rhyme.
5. Reread that stanza out loud.
6. In your workbook write a stanza of the poem with the same rhyme scheme.
   Answer #2: heart, depart

Day 2

1. How are your spelling skills? Use the vowel combinations to complete the words in your workbook. If you can't figure out what the word should be, just start substituting the letters in until a word makes sense.
2. They can be used more than once, so don't cross them off once you've used them.

Day 3

1. Choose a mood to write about.
   - happy, sad, surprised, angry, frustrated, silly, confused, excited...
2. In your workbook make a list of words that describe that feeling, create that feeling, or are synonyms with the mood word you chose.
3. Write a poem in ABABCC format. What does that mean? How many lines? Which rhyme?
4. Write at least one stanza in your workbook. Read your stanza out loud to get the feel of the rhythm of your poem. Do you have lines that are too long? Poems don't just have rhyme; they have rhythm, but more than anything, they have feeling.
5. Use at least three words from your mood-word list.
6. My example follows on the next page.
   - What do you think was my mood and what do you think are the three words from my mood list?

Coming in through the door,
"Long-time, no see," they offer big hugs.
Suitcases laid down on the floor,
They take a seat for fun on the rugs.
All tickles and smiles,
Happy they came the miles.

7. Your poem doesn't have to be perfect, but you have to try your best!
   Answer #3: 6 lines; 1st and 3rd, 2nd and 4th, and last two
   Answer #6: happy, smiles, fun, tickles

Day 4

1. What is the rhyme scheme of the stanza below from the poem, *Children*, by Longfellow?
   - Ye open the eastern windows,
     That look towards the sun,
     Where thoughts are singing swallows
     And the brooks of morning run.
2. In your workbook write a joyful stanza with this rhyme scheme.
   Answer #1: ABCB, Window and swallow have assonance, the same vowel sound, but they aren't exact rhymes.

Day 5

1. Pick a poem from your workbook page.
2. What is its rhyme scheme and rhythm?
3. Write a funny poem with this rhyme scheme.

Day 6

1. There is a phonics practice on your page. Phonics is about sounds. Today you'll be looking at vowel combinations. For instance, look at the similar vowel combinations in each row and notice what sound they make.
   - join, noise, boil
   - meet, feet, greet
   - bail, rain, trait
   - goat, toad, roam
   - proud, cloud, ground
2. You are also going to be identifying parts of speech.
   - noun: person, place, thing
   - pronoun: in the place of a noun
   - verb: action or state of being
   - adjective: describes a noun
   - adverb: describes a verb (or an adjective)

Day 7

1. On your workbook page you'll need to decide between adjective and adverb today. To decide, look at what it's describing.
   - If it is describing a noun, it's an adjective. He did a good job.
   - Adverbs are usually describing verbs. He did the job well.
2. You can also probably hear what sounds right.

Day 8

1. What's the rhyme scheme of this poem?
   - Talk not of sad November, when a day
     Of warm, glad sunshine fills the sky of noon,
     And a wind, borrowed from some morn of June,
     Stirs the brown grasses and the leafless spray. (*Day* by Whittier)
2. For your workbook page, choose a season and describe it in at least one stanza using the same rhyme scheme.
3. Before you write, read this stanza out loud to get the rhythm of the poem.
   Answer #1: ABBA

Day 9

1. Find the rhyme pattern in the poem, *Requirement*, Whittier. It's a little harder because it's not broken into stanzas.
   - We live by Faith; but Faith is not the slave A
     Of text and legend. Reason's voice and God's, B
     Nature's and Duty's, never are at odds. B
     What asks our Father of His children, save A
     Justice and mercy and humility,
     A reasonable service of good deeds,
     Pure living, tenderness to human needs,
     Reverence and trust, and prayer for light to see
     The Master's footprints in our daily ways?
     No knotted scourge nor sacrificial knife,
     But the calm beauty of an ordered life
     Whose very breathing is unworded praise!--
     A life that stands as all true lives have stood,
     Firm-rooted in the faith that God is Good.
2. Where is the exception in the rhyme pattern?
3. On your workbook page you will need to identify the parts of speech and find the adverbs.
   - Remember that adverbs describe verbs or adjectives. They can even describe other adverbs.
     1. We visit often. Often describes visit. (adverb describing verb)
     2. That painting is exceptionally beautiful. Exceptionally is describing beautiful. (adverb describing adjective)

3. He will come very soon. Soon describes come. Very describes soon. (adverb describing adverb)

Answer #1: ABBA, #2 the last two lines

Day 10

1. On your workbook page you will write a psalm that starts each line or most lines with "Praise Him!"
2. Do you need inspiration? Here's Psalm 150.
   - Praise the Lord.

   Praise God in his sanctuary;
   praise him in his mighty heavens.

   Praise him for his acts of power;
   praise him for his surpassing greatness.

   Praise him with the sounding of the trumpet,
   praise him with the harp and lyre,

   praise him with timbrel and dancing,
   praise him with the strings and pipe,

   praise him with the clash of cymbals,
   praise him with resounding cymbals.

   Let everything that has breath praise the Lord.

   Praise the Lord.
   New International Version (NIV)
   Holy Bible, New International Version®, NIV® Copyright ©1973, 1978, 1984, 2011 by Biblica, Inc.® Used by permission. All rights reserved worldwide.

Day 11

1. A **simile** compares two things using the words *like* or *as*.
2. Some examples of similes using "like" are: *sleep like a baby* and *run like the wind*. If you say someone runs like the wind, you are saying they are very fast. You are comparing a person to the wind using the word *like*.
3. Write a simile for cold, soft, and hungry.
4. How long and creative can you make them? You could say, "Hot like fire." Or, you could say, "Hot like a hamburger on a grill at high noon on the fourth of July in Texas." Which is more interesting?
5. Next time you are writing a story and want to say that something or someone was hot, what will you write?
6. You are going to write similes on your worksheet today.

Day 12

1. Read through these examples of similes. These similes use the word *as* to compare.
   - as hungry as a bear
   - proud as a peacock
   - as cheery as the sunshine
   - as plain as day
   - as smooth as silk
2. How would you use these types of similes in a story? She was sentenced to a morning of cleaning her room. As she picked clothes up off the floor, she moved as slow as ….
3. In your workbook you are going to write similes with "as" today.

Day 13

1. Something tangible is physical, literally touchable. The "in" in intangible gives it the opposite meaning.
2. Read this poem. She answers each question (except for the second) with one tangible and one intangible thing.
   - By Rossetti

     What are heavy? Sea-sand and sorrow:
     What are brief? today and tomorrow:
     What are frail? spring blossoms and youth:
     What are deep? the ocean and truth.

3. On your worksheet you will answer questions like these with tangible and intangible answers. There are no right answers.
   - If you can't think up answers to the questions given, then you can use any of your own questions.

   My examples: What are big? the universe and love; What are thieves? jaybirds and worry; What's good medicine? a nap and laughter

Day 14

1. On your worksheet you are going to distinguish between adverbs, verbs, and imperatives. Imperatives are a form of verbs. They are commands. They tell you what to do.
   - Come here.
   - Don't go!
   - Look at this.
   - Wait!
1. Then you will be writing a poem with similes. If you use more than two, get a high five and/or hug. Get a high five and/or hug if you write your own unique similes. And, you can get another bonus high five and/or hug if you write a LONG simile.
2. Remember that similes compare two things using *like* or *as*.

Day 15

1. On your worksheet, you'll be writing a sentence using *intangible*, meaning not physical, can't be touched, and a sentence using *unfettered*, which means unrestrained, nothing's holding you back.
2. Get a high five and/or hug if you can put them both into the same sentence.

Day 16

1. How many lines are in each stanza of *Sympathy* by Dunbar? What is its rhyme scheme?

   I know what the caged bird feels, alas!
   When the sun is bright on the upland slopes;
   When the wind stirs soft through the springing grass
   And the river flows like a stream of glass
   When the first bird sings and the first bud opes,
   And the faint perfume from its chalice steals–
   I know what the caged bird feels!

   I know why the caged bird beats his wing
   Till its blood is red on the cruel bars;
   For he must fly back to his perch and cling
   When he fain would be on the bough a-swing;
   And a pain still throbs in the old, old scars
   And the pulse again with a keener sting–
   I know why he beats his wing!

   I know why the caged bird sings, ah me,
   When his wing is bruised and his bosom sore,
   When he beats his bars and would be free;
   It is not a carol of joy or glee,
   But a prayer he sends from his heart's deep core,
   But a plea that upward to Heaven he flings–
   I know why the caged bird sings!

2. In the workbook you'll write a poem using the same rhyme scheme (meaning you'll write the same number of lines in your stanza) as this poem.
   Answers #1: 7, ABAABCC

Day 17

1. **An-thro-po-morph-ism** is when an unhuman thing acts like it's a person. The easiest example of an-thro-po-morph-ism is any cartoon where an animal acts like it's a person.
2. The easiest way to write **anthropomorphism** is to use the word "I." Write a short "Who Am I" story. Here's my example.

- I sit all day helping others sit. You get to stand and stretch your legs, but I am stuck sitting, sitting, sitting. And not only that, but I give you a nice soft place to sit, and what do I get to sit on? The hard floor! Is that fair? (Who am I?)
3. Here are some grammar reminders before you do your worksheet for today.
   - Subject is the noun the sentence is about. The simple subject is *cup* instead of *the blue cup*.
   - The predicate is the rest of the sentence, what the subject does. The simple predicate is *ran* instead of *ran all the way home*.
   - **Imperative** sentences give a command. **Declarative** sentences make a statement. **Interrogative** sentences ask a question. **Exclamatory** sentences exclaim.
4. When you are finished your worksheet, check your answers. If you got any wrong, GO BACK and look at the right answer and figure out why that answer is right. If you can't figure out why you were wrong, ask for help.

Day 18

1. Take the grammar quiz on your worksheet.
2. When you are finished your worksheet, check your answers. If you got any wrong, GO BACK and look at the right answer and figure out why that answer is right. If you can't figure out why you were wrong, ask for help.

Day 19

1. A **metaphor**, like a simile, is a way to compare two things. A metaphor says one thing IS the other. Here are some examples.
   - Your smile is the sunshine in my day.
   - Life is a rollercoaster.
   - It was a zoo in there.
   - Time is money.
   - That is music to my ears.
   - She is a shining star.
2. Shining comes from the word shine. You drop the E to add –ing onto the end.
3. If I said he had a winning smile, what did I do to the word win to add –ing?
   - I added another N.
4. When you double the consonant like that it keeps that first "i" away from other vowels so that it keeps its short vowel sound. (The "i" short vowel sound is the I sound in the words hit and pick.)
5. To spell shine with an -ing at the end, you drop the "e" and add the –ing. SHINING The second "i" acts like the "e" in shine and makes I say its name.
6. How would you add –ing to these words: hop, hope?
7. Take the grammar quiz on your worksheet.
8. When you are finished your worksheet, check your answers. If you got any wrong, GO BACK and look at the right answer and figure out why that answer is right. If you can't figure out why you were wrong, ask for help.
   Answers #6: hopping, hoping

Day 20

1. Remember: both similes and metaphors compare two things that aren't alike. Similes use "like" or "as." Metaphors say one thing is the other.
2. On your worksheet you will decide if you are looking at a metaphor or simile.
3. If there's enough room for you, write your metaphor using poem on the page. Otherwise you could type it or write it in a notebook.
4. If you use more than one or at least one simile as well, get a high five and/or hug.
5. Read your poem in front of your family.

Day 21

1. You are going to try your hand at two types of poems today.
2. The diamanté is shaped like a diamond. It's the French word for diamond. When you write yours, center it as in the example and try to make it look diamond-shaped. It starts with the subject and then transitions in the middle to another subject, being a sort of opposite of the first.
3. The sensory poem is a poem of similes and metaphors. You are stating what an emotion is like based on the senses.
4. Read the instructions and examples below. In your workbook you'll write one of each today. Can you create a mood or a feeling like these poems?

Diamante

Noun
Two adjectives
Three -ing or -ed ending verbs
Four nouns transitioning subjects
Three -ing or -ed ending verbs
Two adjectives
Noun

(Example - author unknown - edited)
Air
Balmy, Soft
Floating, wafting, soothing
Wind, gale, typhoon, cyclone
Blowing, twisting, howling
Bitter, cold
Blast

Sensory Poem

Choose an emotion
Tell the color of the emotion
Tell the sound of the emotion
Tell the taste of the emotion

Tell the smell of the emotion
Tell the look of the emotion
Tell how it makes you feel

(Example - author unknown)

Anger

Anger is black as midnight.
It sounds like spattering grease.
It tastes like sand in a sandwich,
And smells like a wet dog.
Anger looks like a volcano blowing itself apart.
It makes you feel powerful.

Day 22

1. Today you are going to rhyme. There are three specific rhyming patterns you are going to try today, basically labeled as such by their number of lines. These types of poems often have rhythms as well, but we're focused on rhyming today.
2. Read these explanations and examples and then write a couplet, a triplet, and a quatrain. There's a tip on your worksheet if you are stuck. Also, they can be silly!

Couplets are two lines with rhyming last words.

Why am I on my feet?
I'd rather take a seat!

Triplets have three lines with a rhyming pattern of AAA or ABA.

Can you sit in a chair
Up in the air
While the weather is fair?

Quatrains have four lines with a rhyming pattern of AABB or ABAB.

The Purple Cow by Gelett Burgess

I never saw a purple cow,
I never hope to see one:
But I can tell you, anyhow,
I'd rather see than be one.

Day 23

1. Today in your workbook you are going to write **limericks**.
2. I think these are the most fun to write. They have a rhythm and rhyming pattern.

3. There are five lines: the first two lines and the last line rhyme together and are longer. The middle two lines rhyme with each other and are shorter.
4. In the examples, the underlined syllables are stressed.
   - You can't just stress any syllable. We say words naturally with a stress.
   - Normally we wouldn't say words like AND or TO with an emphasis.
   - We say enJOY; we don't say ENjoy.
   - We say toMORrow; we don't say TOmorrow or tomorROW.
   - Can you hear the rhythm as you read these poems out loud?

   And I would just like to now say
   It's time to go outside to play
   We've been cooped indoors
   Just totally bored
   It's time to enjoy this fine day.

   There was an old man from Peru
   Who dreamed he was eating his shoe
   Awoke in the night
   A terrible fright
   Discovered it totally true. (This one I edited from online – author unknown.)

5. Create two limericks according the rhyme pattern. Match the rhythm scheme as closely as you can. Hint: the classic way to start a limerick is to begin with, "There once was a …," then you can use a noun, often a man, boy, or girl. Then you can use "named or known as" and pick something to get the rhyme you want.

Day 24

1. Today in your workbook you are writing haikus. These are traditional Japanese poems that reflect observations of nature.
2. The format is three lines. There are five syllables in the first and third lines, seven syllables in the second.
3. Read these examples and then write two of your own. The first two are from a famous ancient Japanese poet. They had the right number of syllables in Japanese!

   On a whithered branch
   A crow is sitting
   This autumn eve.

   An old pond!
   A frog jumps in—
   the sound of water.

   Moonlight casts a pale
   blue light on the snow, winter
   perfect, cold and brisk
   (DE LINT, CHARLES - 2002)

Leaf falls from a tree
Lies dead on the hard, cold ground
New life comes in Spring

Day 25

1. In your workbook write a rhyme about something you're learning about in history or science. Include at least two facts.
2. This assignment was inspired by the rhyme, "In fourteen hundred ninety-two Columbus sailed the ocean blue."

Day 26

1. Type out ten of your poems. Work at a computer you can print from. Make sure everything is spelled correctly. Give it to your parents to hold onto. This might be something for your portfolio.
2. Read through this page out loud acting out the different ways to say the sentence. When it writes "quarrel" slanting upwards, that means your voice goes up (like when you ask a question). See if you can follow their directions and make yourself sound excited, surprised, etc. This is from the *New McGuffey Fourth Reader*.

Did the mountain and the squirrel have a quarrel? (Simple question.)

Yes, the mountain and the squirrel had a quarrel. (Indifferent reply; very slight rise.)

Yes, the mountain and the squirrel had a quarrel. (Simple reply.)

Did the mountain and the squirrel have a quarrel? (Astonishment.)

Yes, the mountain and the squirrel had a quarrel. (Positive; finality.)

The mountain and the squirrel had a quarrel! (Excited emphasis.)

The mountain and the squirrel had a quar-rel. (Surprise.)

The mountain and the squirrel had a quar-rel? (Incredulous surprise; circumflex.)

Did the fountain and the squirrel have a quarrel? (Discrimination.)

No, the mountain and the squirrel had a quarrel. (Discrimination.)

Day 27

1. You are going to be taking the things you've learned and putting them into practice. The list of what you need to write examples of is in your workbook.
2. If you need help remembering what they are, you can find simile in Lesson 11, metaphor in Lesson 19, and the rest in Lesson 17.
3. If you can write them into a story, instead of just individual itty bitty examples, get a high five and/or hug.

Day 28

1. In your workbook write an anthropomorphic story. Look around the room you are sitting in. Choose an **inanimate** object, something that's not alive. Write a *short* story as that object. Use the word "I" like that object is the one thinking and speaking in the story.
2. For example, I'll choose the laptop I'm working on. I could write: "All day I'm stared at. How rude is that! If that weren't rude enough, then they sit there and poke at me…"

Day 29

1. Your worksheet today has a spelling activity. Can you figure out what goes in the blank? It would be a good idea to write out any missed word to practice it correctly. Just write it right there in the workbook above the word itself.
2. The second part is for punctuation. Refreshers:
   - Commas come between items in a list, date words or numbers, before quotation marks when needed, and before the conjunction in a compound sentence.
   - Semi-colons can replace periods and are used in lists when commas are used inside the items listed.

Day 30

1. Today you will write a short story in your workbook. A story has a beginning, middle, and end.
2. If you are using an EP reading course, use at least three vocabulary words to get a high five and/or hug.

Day 31

1. In your workbook you are going to identify metaphors today. Remember that a simile uses like or as to compare two unlike things.
2. You also are going to put in commas after introductory phrases. A phrase is a group of words; an introductory phrase is a group of words at the beginning of a sentence. It doesn't actually have to be multiple words. Yes, it can be just one word. (Did you see what I did there?)
   - Every sentence has a comma, so think about where you would naturally pause.
   - After a long prepositional phrase at the beginning of a sentence, there is a comma.
   - To make sure you are putting the comma in the right place, you need to remember that there is never one comma between a subject and its verb.

- Notice, after each comma there is a complete sentence.
- By writing these instructions, I'm really giving you examples.

Day 32

1. Today's worksheet is a quiz on adjectives.
2. You will identify adjectives, use superlative and comparative adjectives correctly, and capitalize proper adjectives. Remember, all names are capitalized.
3. A comparative adjective compares two things. A superlative adjective is when something is the best, the most. When the adjective has three syllables we don't use the endings –er and –est. We say more beautiful or most beautiful, for example.

Day 33

1. Write in the correct word on your worksheet today. These are all verbs and pronouns that are used incorrectly.
2. Singular means one; plural means more than one.
3. It goes every day. They go every day. "It" is singular. "Goes" is the singular form of the verb that matches. "They" is plural. "Go" is the plural form of the verb that matches.
4. We don't think about singular and plural when we speak and write. It just comes naturally if English is your first language. When you go to learn a foreign language and find out that the verb changes based on who is doing it, remember that we do that in English too. You just don't notice!

Day 34

1. Today's worksheet is a little quiz covering several topics. Here are some reminders.
   - The simple subject is the noun that the sentence is about.
   - The simple predicate is the verb that goes with the subject.
   - A contraction combines two words, replacing some letters. I am becomes I'm.
   - An action verb is something you do. A linking verb links two things together. I am happy. I = happy. The kitten feels soft. The kitten = soft. I feel the squishy mud under my feet. I = mud. No, that one is not a linking verb!

Day 35

1. In your workbook write a short story using at least one simile and one metaphor. Get a high five and/or hug if you use more.
2. Don't forget to end your story!

Day 36

1. You are going to start writing a five-paragraph essay.
2. Choose a topic from history or science to write about. Maybe you could use something you are learning about right now.
3. Use your worksheet for today to write a fact about your topic in each petal.

Day 37

1. Do you remember what the five paragraphs to a short essay are?
   - introduction
   - 3 body paragraphs
   - conclusion
2. Today choose your three main points. To do that look at your facts. Can they be organized into three topics? If one doesn't fit, it's okay to leave it out. You need at least two facts for each point you want to make.
   - Write what your three points are going to be. For instance, for an essay on the pyramids write, "1. The pyramids were made by workers, not slaves."
   - Then write the number 1 on the petal facts that would go with that topic. (Example: 1. Workers were paid with bread and beer.)
3. There is also a little spelling activity on your worksheet page. Here are some reminders.
   - Words ending in sh, s, ch, x, or z usually become plural by adding ES.
   - Words ending in a consonant and then the letter Y become plural by changing the Y into an I and adding ES.

Day 38

1. Write your introduction. There is no worksheet page for this. I suggest typing it so that you can edit it easily. We'll be working on this for several days.
2. The first sentence should catch the reader's attention. Use a strange fact or ask a question or use an interesting quote. Then say something about your topic but don't give your facts yet. The last sentence is your **thesis statement**, your **topic sentence**. This sentence tells what your essay is going to be about. Don't write, "My essay is about…"
3. Here's an example.
   - You've seen pictures of pyramids, right? Did you know that each stone in a pyramid weighed as much as a car? The pyramids were built with a lot of hard work, but also with a lot of intelligence. The pyramids were an amazing feat of engineering.
4. Did I get you interested with my questions and an interesting fact?
5. What is my **thesis** or **main topic**?
   - answer: The pyramids are an amazing feat of engineering.
6. On your workbook page correct the mistakes in capitalization, punctuation, spelling, and word choice.

Day 39

1. Today write one of your middle paragraphs. Decide what order they will go in to make the most sense.
   - There is not room for this in your workbook. Do this on a computer if you can to practice your typing and to make it easier for editing.
2. Your first sentence should be your **topic sentence**, your main point.
   - Ex. You might imagine that the pyramids were made by slaves, but really they were built by paid workers.

3. Then you write your facts. Try to write three sentences for this part, but I would rather you write two long sentences than three short ones.
4. Next you write your conclusion sentence.
   - Ex. Pyramid workers not only were not slaves, but they had comfortable lives and also the noble purpose of serving their king.
5. On your worksheet there is a pronoun activity. This is mostly about subject and object pronouns. Here's a reminder.
   - I is a subject pronoun. You use it when you are the one doing the action. I like to play basketball.
   - Me is the object pronoun. You use it when you are receiving the action and after prepositions. Come with me. Give it to me.
   - If there is another name with I or me, the same thing applies. If you are unsure, just take out the other name. Antoinette and me live on the same street. You wouldn't say, "Me live on the same street as her." It's Antoinette and I live on the same street.

Day 40

1. On your worksheet you'll be writing similes.
2. A simile is a comparison of two unlike things using like or as.
   - I'm as exhausted as a triathlete finishing a race.

Day 41

1. There are two spelling activities on your worksheet today.

Day 42

1. Complete the worksheet on object and subject pronouns.
   - Subject pronouns are the ones that come before verbs such as I sing, you laugh, he dances, she plays, it works, we live, and they have.
   - Object pronouns come after the verb such as give him, write her, call them, and bring us.
2. Today write the next of your middle paragraphs. Below are the directions I gave you on Day 39.
   - Your first sentence should be your **topic sentence**, your main point. (Ex. You might imagine that the pyramids were made by slaves, but really they were built by paid workers.)
   - Then you write your facts. Try to write three sentences for this part, but I would rather you write two long sentences than three short ones.
   - Then you write your conclusion sentence.

Day 43

1. On your worksheet you'll be choosing the correct pronoun.
2. Today write the last of your middle paragraphs. You can see the directions above in Day 42.

Day 44

1. Complete the verb quiz in your workbook. You will be choosing the correct past tense form of the verb. Past tense is the form we use when talking about something that's happened already.
2. Today write your conclusion, the last paragraph of your essay.
   - The *first* sentence of your conclusion should retell your **thesis statement** or **topic sentence** from your introduction. DON'T just copy the sentence, though. Tell it in new words.
   - Your paragraph should have at least three sentences.
   - The last sentence of the paragraph should tell us why you wrote about it, what's so important about this, why should we care about this…Make some sort of statement. Here's my example of a conclusion.
     - The pyramids are remarkable considering the time period in which they were built. Other cultures remained primitive while the Egyptians were engineering colossal wonders. I think the pyramids prove that God was right when he decided to confuse the languages of the people on earth. He said, "Nothing they plan to do will be impossible for them." (Genesis 11:6b NIV1984)

Day 45

1. Edit your essay. Use the editing checklist in your workbook.
2. It's a good idea to read what you wrote out loud. Anywhere you stumble, you should make a change. Something wasn't right.
3. Add a title, your name, and the date. Print your essay when you are sure it's your best. Give it to your parents to add to your portfolio.

Day 46

1. On your worksheet for today there is an alphabetical order activity.
   - You compare the first letter of the words. Whichever word begins with the letter that comes first in the alphabet comes first in alphabetical order.
   - If their first letters match, look at the next letter to see which comes first.
2. There are also sentences on the page. Or are there? A sentence has a subject and a predicate. The subject is who is doing or being the predicate, the verb part of the sentence.
   - You'll need to transform any incomplete sentences into sentences. Are they missing the subject or the verb, the predicate? Add in what's missing.

Day 47

1. Today you will be writing a dialogue, a discussion between two people, well, two animals in this case. There is a page for this in your workbook.
2. You need to use speech tags to show who is talking.
   - "Psst. Come here!" the snake hissed.
   - "Why?" the sheep inquired.
   - "I have something to show you," the snake said.
   - The sheep asked, "What is it?"
3. You can use my example for a reminder of dialogue punctuation. Also notice that the subject comes before the verb in the speech tag. I wrote, "The snake hissed," not "hissed the snake."
4. It is okay to use said. You will see in the books you read that authors use said. If they said it, they *said* it. But if they answered or whispered or retorted or yelled, then say so.
5. Try to use words other than said in each dialogue you write. Here are some ideas: whispered, yelled, explained, remarked, cried, demanded, agreed, warned.

Day 48

1. There are two pages in your workbook for today. There is one for writing a dialogue between two characters in history. King Tut and Neil Armstrong…whomever you like.
2. Before you do that, review your dialogue punctuation. Check your answers before you write your dialogue so you know you got it.
   - Punctuation always comes before the quotation marks.
   - Sentences inside the quotes end with a !, ? or , not a period if it is followed by a speech tag.
   - The speech tag doesn't have a capital letter if it's not starting the sentence.

Day 49

1. When there is a speech tag in the middle of the quotation, it follows the same rules. The trick is that if the second part is its own sentence, then it is preceded by a period and begins with a capital letter. If it's not its own sentence but a continuation of the same sentence, it's preceded by a comma and does not begin with a capital letter.
   - This isn't that tricky really. A sentence starts with a capital letter and ends with a period. We never put a period and capital letter in the middle of any sentence.
2. On your worksheet for today, first you'll practice with the punctuation of in-the-middle speech tags, and then you will write a dialogue between you and someone in your family, or really anyone. The point is to write correct dialogue.
3. One more dialogue rule to remember. Each speaker begins a new paragraph. That means it begins on a new line and is indented, moved over. (You can look in a book if you don't know what I mean.)

Day 50

1. Write a fable, a little tale, with the moral, "It's what's on the inside that counts."
2. That means your story should teach a lesson. I'm giving you the lesson it's supposed to teach. The moral is related to the idea that you shouldn't judge a book by its cover.

Day 51

1. Today we're talking about the parts of a story.
   - Setting
     - The setting is the where and when a story takes place.
       - on Mars in the distant future
       - in your home today
       - in a castle a thousand years ago
     - Don't forget to make sure your audience knows the time and place in your story. You don't have to just tell them. You can show them by how you describe the place and what's happening there.
   - Characters
     - The characters are the who in your story. There is a main character that the story is about and there are supporting characters.
     - Usually there is a hero and a villain, the good guy and the bad guy.
       - The hero is called the protagonist. We root for the good guy to get what he is after and to have a happy ending.
       - The villain is called the antagonist. The antagonist tries to stop the main character from being happy and succeeding at getting whatever they are after.
       - There can be more than hero and villain.
     - In your stories you need to describe the characters. Your readers need to know what they look like, how old they are, and what they are like. You don't have to just tell them. You can show them by the things they do in the story.
   - Plot
     - The plot is the what of the story. It's the action. It's what takes place.
     - This is what gives your story a beginning, middle, and end.
     - The beginning is called the exposition.
       - It sets the stage. It gives background information on the characters and the setting. What's been going on before the story begins, where the characters find themselves, and why etc.
     - The middle is the conflict. You don't have a story if there is no conflict.
       - The hero needs to want something. The conflict is that the hero wants it and the villain is trying to stop the hero from getting it.
       - The more it looks like the hero can't possibly accomplish their goal, the more exciting the story is.
       - The conflict is a question. Will she or won't she? Can he or can't he? We know the answer will be yes, they can and they will, but

the more it looks like the answer might be they can't and the won't, the more interesting your story will be.

- The end has two parts, the climax and the resolution.
    - The climax is the end of the exciting conclusion. It's when the question finally gets answered. They did it!
    - The resolution is the wrapping of the story.
        - It's the warm and fuzzy happy ending.
        - It shows us what happens next. Here are some examples.
            - They all hug and now they are friends. They go on to compete at a higher level. They get married and live happily ever after.

2. In your workbook answer the questions about the parts of a story.

Day 52

1. Today you will be practicing subjects and predicates.
2. The simple subject and predicate are often just one word.
    - The simple subject is the noun that the sentence is about.
    - The simple predicate is the verb that goes with the subject.
3. Everything in a sentence is part of either the complete subject or the complete predicate.
    - The complete subject is everything the sentence is about. It's the noun and everything that modifies it.
    - The complete predicate is everything else in the sentence.
    - Example
        - The big red, juicy apple sits on the counter.
            - Complete subject is "the big red, juicy apple."
            - Compete predicate is "sits on the counter."
            - Simple subject is "apple."
            - Simple predicate is "sits."
    - Example
        - The basket of apples on the counter is full.
            - Complete subject is "the basket of apples on the counter."
            - Complete predicate is "is full."
            - Simple subject is "basket."
            - Simple predicate is "is."
4. Identify the subjects and predicates on your worksheet for today.

Day 53

1. On your spelling worksheet for today. You have to identify short vowel sounds.
    - The short a sound is the sound of A in hat.
    - The short e sound is the sound of E in pet.
    - The short I sound is the sound of I in hit.
    - The short u sound is the sound of U in hut.

2. There is a second page in your workbook. You are to write a paragraph about how you would come up with money if you needed some fast.
   - Make sure to start your paragraph explaining what you are going to be writing about. The person you give your paragraph to may have not read this assignment and may have no idea what you are talking about.
     - If I needed to come up with money fast, I would first…
   - Come up with two ways–one reasonable, one crazy.

Day 54

1. There is a spelling worksheet in your workbook using the words from Day 53.
2. There is a second page for today. Write a short story (it can be just one paragraph) about a problem and how you solved it. It can be anything from getting gum stuck on your shoe to being new and not having any friends.
3. You are going to come back to this, so if you type it, make sure you save it somewhere you can find it.

Day 55

1. Read this sample story written by a fifth grader. You'll find it below. It also has the teacher's comments in different categories. Pay attention to the corrections given by the teacher! They will make your writing better.
2. What was good and what was not good about the story?
3. There is no workbook page today.

A Horrible Day

Have you ever sufferd so much pain in your life. I have and it wasnt pretty.

It started out like the most wonderful day of my life. It was the last day of fourth grade and my whole class was excited and sad at the same time but we had a water fight so when I got home I needed to switch my clothes since I was soackend wet, and I remembered that my mom had bought me some new sandles. I placed them on and rushed out to go enough myself out side.

When I got outside every body was around the tallest smootheist tree shouting the cats goinog to fall!!! So I rushed over there to see and found out that it was my little kitty so I tried to climb up to get it, but since the tree was slippery I slipped and landed on my poor hand I felt a crack.

I cried and cried that it was like a river of tears. My mom came out crying because she heard what happened so she drove me to the hospital as quickly as she could, but every time she would turn I would feel my bone, kept craking and I couldent stop crying. When I got to the hospital I had to wait a long time, but still I couldent stop crying.

finally when the doctor saw me He took x-rays of my arm and told me it was broken I cried even stronger. They put on a tempory cast just for the mean time and told my mom to make a apomeint.

When it was time for my apomeint I went in speedy quick. I have always wondered what it would be like having a cast and I knew I was going to get one today. I got to select the color of cast of course I elected pink. When I was getting my cast I saw pictures of what happendes if I get my cast wet. So I got very frightened and I was never close to getting in the water.

The whole summer I was in my room really bored and hot, but I didn't want to get my skin wet either way and I lasted one whole month like that.

When it was finally the day to get my cast off I was so cheerful. When I saw what they were going to use got terrified and the whole I was hitting the doctor because I was really frightened. The doctor said that I looked like I was catching flies. When it was finally over my hand felt weak. I couldent do anything with it.

When I finally wanted to play It was time to go back to school I was furious. So this summer I am going to observe myself very carefully so I wont Break a bone again. Every summer something happens to me, but not this summer. At least I hope nothing happens to me.

Commentary (notes from the teacher about the writing in this story)

Ideas/Content
The writer develops the central idea of pain and suffering by relating a personal experience of breaking an arm. The writer relates the central idea though the setting, events, conflict, resolution, and insights into the character.

Organization
•The introduction invites the reader into the piece with an engaging hook (i.e., "Have you ever suffered so much pain in your life? I have and it wasn't pretty.").
• The conclusion wraps up the story in a satisfying manner and includes the writer's reflection on the personal importance of the story (i.e., "So this summer I am going to observe myself very carefully so I won't break a bone again.").
• Description of the events clearly establishes the situation and emotional reaction of the character. Example: outside by tree, cat trapped in tree, fall from the tree, broken hand.
• The sequential structure is appropriate for the genre and supportive of the reader.

Voice
• The writer's voice is evident in the piece (i.e., "I have always wondered what it would be like having a cast and I knew I was going to get one today. I got to select the color of cast of course I selected pink." "I lasted one whole month like that.").
• The story is told effectively through the first person Word and Language Choice
• The writer includes some precise words (i.e. rushed, soaked, suffered, cracking).
• The writer includes some descriptive phrases/figurative language to show the reader rather then just tell (i.e., "…it was like a river of tears." "When I saw what they were going to use [to remove the cast, I] got terrified and the whole [time] I was hitting the doctor because I was really frightened. The doctor said that I looked like I was catching flies.").

Sentence Fluency
• Sentences are well built with strong and varied structure and length.
• Transitional expressions link sentences and paragraphs (i.e., finally, but then it started out). The writer over-relies on the word when.

Written English
Language Conventions
Numerous errors in spelling, grammar, and punctuation impede the reader and impact the meaning.

Writing sample and remarks from: "Samples of Proficient Writing with Commentaries Grade 5," San Diego Unified School District, Office of the Deputy Superintendent, Instruction and Curriculum Division, Literacy and History-Social Science Department, 2006

Day 56

1. Complete the spelling activity in your workbook. This time it talks about long vowels.
   - The long vowel sound is when the vowels (A E I O U) say their names.
   - A as in day
   - E as in tea
   - I as in high
   - O as in goat
   - U as in blue
2. Read the sample story written by a fifth grader. It also has the teacher's comments in different categories. Pay attention to the corrections given by the teacher! They will make your writing better.
3. What did the student do well? What could the student have done better?

Dancing

I walk on. Stomp! I hit my pose. I hear the music. "Ease on down, ease on down the road." It has started. I turn around and I'm off. I know it so well I could do it with my eyes closed. I smile big and do all the facial exspetions my teacher has taught me. I think back. How did I start? How did I get this far?

"I don't want to go!" My mom's friend Mellisa was taking her niece to dance and asked me to come along. I was a three year old having a fit out in front. I hated the idea of trying something new. I would rather be at home. In class we tried some things. My favorite part was when we put ballet shoes on and skiped around the room. I liked it but, I still did not want to come back. Bu the time the reciatal cam, I loved it. I knew the whole dance by heart just like I do now. I kept going till I was 5. We were moving and I could not dance anymore. When I started school my friend started dance with me. It was fun to have a friend with me. just my luck my friend did not like it and I was alone again. My mom worked with a lady that has a daughter that helps teach classes at a studio. Believe it or not, she is now my teacher. My mom takes me their and I love it. Everyone is so nice. I keep going and going. Each recial I get better and better. Each compatition my dance gets better and better ratings.

Each year we have different coustumes and different songs. No two dances are ever the same. There are so many really good teachers that come up with some creative moves and formations. I think it would be neat to be a teacher. Making up dances, picking out songs, and best of all, designing coustumes. When I'm 16 I want to get a part time job at my studio. It would be so fun just to help.

It's almost the end. I hit my pose and yell "Yah". There is a huge appulusule. The judges nodd to each other and scribble down on their papers. I take a bow and walk off. I am pround of myself and I am pround I am a dancer.

Commentary
Ideas/Content
The writer establishes character around a central idea (i.e., not liking to dance at first and being very comfortable with dancing now). The writer begins sharing her thoughts as she is

dancing, flashes back to beginning her dance classes, and concludes the writing by finishing her dance confidently from the beginning of the piece. Writing Strategies

Organization
• The writer engages the reader by jumping right into the action. The writer provides sufficient context, using a very rhythmic text, to support the reader's understanding (i.e., "I walk on. Stomp! I hit my pose. I hear the music. "Ease on down, ease on down the road." It has started. I turn around and I'm off. I know it so well I could do it with my eyes closed.").
• The writer crafts the conclusion to echo the temporal setting of the introduction. The ending thought is somewhat detached from the action (i.e., "I am proud of myself and I am proud I am a dancer.").
• The writer effectively transitions from the present to the past (i.e., dancing right now, threw a fit like a 3 year old, danced until age 5, went to school, at 16, dancing now). The writer's flashback in time is creative and purposeful to the genre and clear to the reader.

Voice
• The writer's voice is authentic and confident. (i.e., "I smiled big." "I was alone again." "I hit my pose." "I'm proud of myself and I am a dancer.").
• The writer uses the first person to convey the narrative.

Word and Language Choice
• The writer's choice of words and phrases is appropriate to the purpose and considerate of the audience.
• The writer uses topic-specific language that adds authenticity and clarity to the piece (i.e., stomp, costumes, pose, formation, creative moves).

Sentence Fluency
• Sentences vary in length and structure. Dialogue is used sparingly but effectively.
• Sentences and paragraphs are well connected through the use of transitional devices (i.e., flashback) and transitional terms (i.e., by the time, when, when I started, each year, it's almost the end).

Language Conventions
Spelling, grammars, and punctuation are mostly correct.

Writing sample and remarks from: "Samples of Proficient Writing with Commentaries Grade 5," San Diego Unified School District, Office of the Deputy Superintendent, Instruction and Curriculum Division, Literacy and History-Social Science Department, 2006

Day 57

1. Complete the spelling page in your workbook.
2. Read the writing sample by a fifth grader. This isn't a story. This is writing about a book the student has read. Pay attention to the corrections given by the teacher! They will make your writing better.
3. What did the student do well? What could the student have done better?

Literature Response, *Returns Again*

This is a story of a Lakota warrior's son. The warrior, Returns Again, got his name by winning a battle for his people when everyone was frightened. On the other hand, his sone was observed to be taking a long time in everything he did. Therefore, his family names him Slon-he which means slow. Slow could never measure up to his father with a name like "Slow". Can you imagine how Slow felt.

Compared to his father, Slow felt ashamed of his name. What's in a name you ask? During those times a name tells about a person's character, reputation, and how a person acted. He didn't want to be called "Slow" forever. Slow knew that he had to do something about his name. But in order to change his name he had to do a great deed, so he wished for all this to come true.

Finally, Slow's wish came true. First, he made an effort to change the meaning of his name. The new meaning to his name means determination and courage. But did he ever accomplish his goal on changing his name.

If you think making a difference is easy, think again. When Slow was about seven everyone knew him as one of the strongest boys among them all. Slow was only ten when he caught his first baby buffalo. Till then nobody has been making fun of him, but his name was still the same. Now fourteen, Slow had a great opportunity to change his name. Slow became a hero by making the Crow warriors run away. Slow's father, Returns Again, changed his name to Tatan'ka Iyota'ke which means Sitting Bull-one of the highest of the whole Lakota warriors. Since then he is now known as Sitting Bull.

After all that Sitting Bull did, he became a brave, heroic, and respected by his people. His family also changed their opinion of Slow that they even gave him a new name. His people changed by not making fun of him and by giving him more respect. You see a lot of people changed. That's what I call making a real difference.

One thing I'll always keep is that you have to earn the things that you want. One example is that you have to do your homework before you get to do anything else. Or like Sitting Bull, he had to do great deeds to change his name.

"The best way," Returns Again told him "to gain respect of your people is to be both brave and wise." - Returns Again Page 12

Commentary

Ideas/Content

The writer clearly states the central idea of the piece in the first paragraph (i.e., "Slow could never measure up to his father with a name like 'Slow'") and identifies both the character and context of the story.

Analysis

Throughout the piece, the writer explores the character's problem (i.e., "…his son was observed to be taking a long time in everything he did." "Slow felt ashamed of his name." "Slow knew that he had to do something about his name."). The writer describes key events to describe the character's determination to resolve his problem (i.e., "First, he made an effort to change the meaning of his name." "Slow was only ten when he caught his first baby buffalo.")

Interpretation
The writer interprets the text to develop the central idea around the importance of earning respect. The writer relates multiple events that describe how Slow became a hero and how he earned the respect of his people (i.e., interaction with Crow warriors, first baby buffalo, changing his name).

Organization
• The structure is appropriate for the purpose and supportive of the reader.
• The writer introduces the context and central idea in the first paragraph; develops this central idea in subsequent paragraphs with appropriate facts and details; and crafts an interpretative conclusion that supports the central idea.

Voice
• The writer's voice is apparent as he speaks to the reader (i.e., "Can you imagine how..." "One thing I'll always keep..." "That's what I call...").
• The writer respects/admires the character's tenacity, focus, and impact (i.e., "You see a lot of people changed [as a result of Sitting Bull's actions]. That's what I call making a real difference.").

Word and Language Choice
• The writer's word and language choices adequately convey meaning, however the language palette is nonspecific and somewhat limited.
• While not vivid, the descriptions are functional (i.e., "Slow felt ashamed of his name." "Slow had a great opportunity to change his name.").

Sentence Fluency
• The writer uses appropriate transitional expressions (i.e., "Compared to his father... ," "Since then he is... ," "After all that …"). The writer uses variation in sentence structure.
• The writer uses a variety of transitional words and phrases that move the reader through the piece (i.e., on the other hand, therefore, during those times, finally, first, when slow was about seven, now fourteen).

Conventions
Spelling and punctuation are generally correct.

Writing sample and remarks from: "Samples of Proficient Writing with Commentaries Grade 5," San Diego Unified School District, Office of the Deputy Superintendent, Instruction and Curriculum Division, Literacy and History-Social Science Department, 2006

Day 58

1. An **independent clause** is a group of words that express a complete thought. A simple sentence is an independent clause.
   • I like pizza
   • That phrase can stand independently on its own. It's an independent clause.
2. A **dependent clause** is a group of words that cannot stand on its own. It may have a subject and a verb, but it depends on another clause to make a complete sentence.

- When you get home
- That clause does not stand on its own. It's missing something. It needs an independent clause to come along aside it to turn it into a complete sentence.

3. A **compound sentence** is when two independent clauses are joined together with a conjunction. A comma is usually placed before the conjunction.
    - I like pizza, but I also like chicken noodle soup.
    - Would you like pizza, or would you like soup?
        - Each half of the sentence is an independent clause. "I like pizza" stands on its own independently, and "I also like chicken noodle soup" stands on its own independently.

4. A **complex sentence** is when a dependent and independent clause are combined into a sentence.
    - *If you come now,* you'll be able to see it.
    - I don't want to *because I don't like that.*
        - In the examples, I underlined the independent clauses and put the dependent clauses in italics.
        - Read each clause and make sure you can recognize that it can stand on its own (independent) or that it can't stand on its own (dependent).

5. You will be identifying and writing compound and complex sentences in your workbook today.

Day 59

1. Your **voice** as a writer is the way you sound when you write. Your voice can be humorous, serious, exciting, or boring.
2. A strong voice means interesting writing. To have a stronger voice choose interesting words and descriptions. Don't say you are happy. Say you feel like you could fly. Don't say you were excited. Say you were shaking, unable to contain all the excitement you were feeling.
3. You also need to match your tone to the style of writing. If you are writing a letter to the president, you would use a different tone than if you were writing a letter to a friend.
4. Complete your worksheet on voice. A personal narrative is a story about something that happened to you.

Day 60

1. Could you write a compound and complex sentence? If you don't remember what those are, take a look back at Day 58. You may need to know for your worksheet today.
2. The main topic of your workbook page today is word choice. The emphasis is on choosing specific words. Don't say, whisper. Don't run, sprint. Don't go to the store, go to Walmart. Don't pet your dog, pet your beagle. Don't eat dinner, eat chicken dumplings. Get the idea?

Day 61

1. There is a spelling page in your workbook today. Pay attention as you write the words. This is to help you, but you need to keep your brain engaged!
2. There is a second page in your workbook. Score your short story about the problem you solved (Day 54). Check off which comment matches your story in each category.

Day 62

1. Complete the spelling page in your workbook.
2. Rewrite your short story. Fix all the problems so that it would get a perfect score.

Day 63

1. Read this research report by a fifth grader. Pay attention to the corrections given by the teacher! They will make your writing better.
2. What did the student do well? What could the student have done better?

Helping Elephants to Survive

Picture the scene. Thousands of hacked up bodies of gentle giants as they all are being slaughtered away for land. Ruthless humans take away all the land for their greedy selves. Many people slaughter thousands and thousands of elephants to solve the overpopulation of land. Some people are making new environments for many elephants to live in because they are in danger. The humans will kill as many elephants they want so there is more land for the humans. The governments should be caring for elephants and other endangered animals.

Some people are making new environments for elephants to live in because they are in danger. The animals that are in danger need to live in a safe environment away from poachers and hunters. Most conservationists think that the only way elephants can survive being poached for their ivory is to stop the ivory trade from going on. When the conservationists try to build new reserves it becomes harder each time to build. It is hard because the humans that live on that land have crops growing there. One conservation group called the African Elephant Conservation Trust is helping the elephants survive by making more reserves. Also other people around the world like conservationists and scientists are trying to help the elephants survive. The elephant population is becoming a big deal to many conservationists and they will try to stop poachers from poaching animals around the world.

I think that it is finally great that more people are helping animals that are endangered. There also needs to be a new place where the elephants have enough room to lie in and can be safe at the same time.

The humans will kill as many elephants as they want so there is more ivory for the ivory trade and more land for the humans. What people can do to help the elephant future become better is to stop buying ivory products. There are conservationist groups who think that the future for the elephants is bad because to many poachers are poaching them for more land. Many farmers will kill the elephants because they are afraid that the elephants will kill them first. Masai herdsmen also kill elephants to protect their grass for their own cattle to survive.

A lot of conservationist groups want more people to help the elephants so the future of the elephants will become better. Because elephants are being slaughtered for land, there are now fewer elephants than in the past year. If no one continue to help, more of the elephants might become extinct.

I think that, if people don't help animals they could all be gone forever. The people should at least try to give more land for animals to live in. I was surprised to learn that so many elephants are being slaughtered and we only have about 50,000 left of them on earth.

The governments should be caring for elephants and other endangered animals. Michael Fay, an elephant researcher wants to investigate more to help stop elephant slaughter. Some governments are going against poaching because the elephant population might become extinct. Several countries are banning raw ivory and other ivory products from crossing their countries. African countries like Zimbabwe have many elephants and they are building several reserves to keep the elephants safe. However, some governments that are poor still slaughter elephants to pay for guns and other fire arms. Conservationist and other people also try to help the elephants by using the money from tourism they get.

I think that the government needs to be more responsible and make more laws to stop poaching. There should be more reserves for animals and more people helping. I think that banning ivory trade is good because the elephants might be able to live longer.

Humans that do not care for elephants are killing gentle and harmless elephants, just to solve the over population problem on the land. The people that care for elephants like scienctists are helping more to save the elephants from being wiped off the face of this planet.

Ideas/Content
The writer develops a central idea to support a self-directed investigation of how to help elephants survive.

Support
• The writer provides information to support the idea that elephants could become endangered or that they are a threatened species (i.e., development of their natural environment, ivory trade, farm land, poachers).
• The writer cites topical experts (i.e., "Michael Fay, an elephant researcher …") and includes four references on the bibliography. There is no evidence of the use of technology to locate or present information.

Elaboration
• The writer effectively explains information that supports the central idea. The writer shares multiple examples of what is currently being done to help elephants survive (i.e., African Elephant Conservation group, Zimbabwe, Michael Fay-elephant researcher) and offers some personal suggestions about how the government could help elephants survive (i.e., Zimbabwe animal reserves, tourism money).

Organization
• The writer engages the reader in the introduction by describing a specific scene that shows the situation many elephants face (i.e., "Picture the scene. Thousands of hacked up bodies of gentle giants as they all are being slaughtered away for land."). The introduction delineates the problem (i.e., "Many people slaughter thousands and thousands of elephants to solve the

overpopulation of land."), current strategies for supporting the survival of elephants (i.e., "Some people are making new environments for many elephants to live in because they are in danger."), and a call for action (i.e., "The governments should be caring for elephants and other endangered animals.).
• The conclusion provides a sense of closure and resolution.
• The overall structure is appropriate to the purpose and showcases the central idea.

Voice
• The writer's voice is appropriate to the audience and purpose. Sometimes the writer speaks directly to the reader (i.e., "Picture the scene. Thousands of hacked up bodies of gentle giants as they all are being slaughtered away for land.") and other times the writer's voice is appropriately detached (i.e., "One conservation group called the African Elephant Conservation Trust is helping the elephants survive by making more reserves.").
• The writer's point of view is abundantly clear (i.e., "Ruthless humans take away all the land for their greedy selves." "I think that it is finally great that more people are helping animals that are endangered." "I think that the government needs to be more responsible and make more laws to stop poaching.").

Word and Language Choice
The writer uses topic-specific language (i.e., poacher, endangered, reserves, ivory, conservationists, investigate), persuasive language (i.e., overpopulation, ruthless, slaughtered, gentle giants, greedy selves, wiped off the face of this planet) to enhance/develop the central idea.

Sentence Fluency
• The writer uses some variation in sentence structure.
• Sentences and paragraphs are effectively connected.

Conventions
Spelling, grammar, and punctuation are mostly correct.

Writing sample and remarks from: "Samples of Proficient Writing with Commentaries Grade 5," San Diego Unified School District, Office of the Deputy Superintendent, Instruction and Curriculum Division, Literacy and History-Social Science Department, 2006

Day 64

1. We're going to keep learning about sentences. Today's lesson is on sentences that aren't really sentences.
2. There are two types we talk about: **run-on sentences** and **sentence fragments**.
   - A run-on sentence is when more than one sentence is smooshed together.
     - I love dogs I would have a million if I could.
       - That's really two sentences. I love dogs. I would have a million if I could.
   - A sentence fragment is just a sentence part, not the whole thing.
     - Ready or not.
     - That's not a complete sentence. There is no subject and verb.
3. Complete the worksheet by recognizing and fixing the run-ons and fragments.

Day 65

1. Possessives show ownership. That is my ball. It is Jerome's bat.
2. Apart from possessive pronouns like my and your, we use an apostrophe to show possession.
3. To show that the collar belongs to the cat, we write that it's the cat's collar.
   - You add an apostrophe and the letter S.
4. The only trick here is that if the word is plural and ends with an S already, you don't add an extra S. You just write the apostrophe.
   - boys, girls, children
   - boys' game, girls' game, children's game
5. You will be practicing this on our worksheet for today.

Day 66

1. Complete the spelling activity in your workbook and write possessives.
2. Look back at Day 65 if you need a reminder.

Day 67

1. Complete your workbook page by doing the spelling activity and writing a description.
2. Use great words!

Day 68

1. An adverb tells when, where, or how something was done. They are used in describing verbs, but can also describe adjectives. That was really hard!
2. You are going to make the sentences on your worksheet better today by adding and taking away adverbs.

Day 69

1. Here's a reminder of comma rules.
   - separate items in a list of three or more
   - before a conjunction that joins independent clauses
   - after a dependent clause connected to an independent clause
   - separate out phrases that are additional, not essential to the meaning
   - separate an introductory element from the rest of the sentence
   - between city and country, state, or province
   - between date numbers and words
   - separating quotes and speech tags
2. On your worksheet you'll choose the sentences that correctly use commas.

Day 70

1. You are going to write a little story today. Follow the directions. It's to make sure you use lots of commas to practice!
2. Get a high five and/or hug if you use at least five comma rules.

Day 71

1. Follow the directions and complete the spelling worksheet. There are many different ways to write the "er" sound.
2. Pay attention to how the words are written differently even though they have the same sound.

Day 72

1. Look at these examples:
   - The dog chased my brother and ____.
     - What goes in the blank, me or I? An easy way to check is by taking out the extra person.
     - The dog chased ____.
       - Now it's easy to know the answer, right?
   - Try it the other way. Read the sentence below. Should you add in I or me?
     - My brother and ____ ran home.
       - Take away the extra person.
       - ____ ran home.
       - Now you know!
2. This is what you'll be doing on your worksheet today. Take out the extra words.
   Answers #1: The dog chased my brother and me. My brother and I ran home.

Day 73

1. Today you are going to write a summary of a novel you have recently finished reading. This is going to become part of a book review. Type your summary and SAVE IT! When there is the same writing assignment over several days, there is no workbook page. I do recommend typing this if you are able.
2. When you write your summary, it should be in the *present* tense.
   - Here's an example of the present tense: In the beginning of the story life <u>is </u>happy for Cinderella, but then her father <u>dies</u>. Her stepmother <u>makes</u> her a slave to the family.
   - This is the same thing in past tense. (Don't do this!): In the beginning of the story life <u>was</u> happy for Cinderella, but then her father <u>died</u>. Her stepmother <u>made</u> her a slave to the family.

Day 74

1. You have a workbook page today where you will rewrite the paragraph and replace the underlined words with their synonyms from the box. Make sure to alter the verbs to be in the correct tense.
   - A synonym is a word of similar meaning.
   - If writing a lot is physically hard for you, you can ask a parent nicely if you can just write the replacement words or if you could type the paragraph.
2. Next, you need to work on your book review from Day 73. After your summary, which you already wrote, write two reasons why you liked the book.
   - Write your reasons as topic sentences, the first sentence of a paragraph. In *The Book Title* the author….
     - You will be writing your paragraphs on Day 75. Today you are writing your topic sentences and thinking up examples from the book that show what you are talking about.
     - It would be a good idea to type out your sentences to make it easier for you to use them on Day 75.

Day 75

1. You are going to continue working on your book review. Start with your two topic sentences from Day 74. These are not in your workbook. You should have this saved somewhere.
2. You are going to turn each of your topic sentences into a paragraph.
3. Follow each reason with at least one example from the book that shows what you are talking about.
4. Write a concluding sentence to each paragraph stating how the example shows the point you are trying to make.
5. You should have two paragraphs written when you are done.

Day 76

1. Write an introduction and conclusion for your book review.
2. The last sentence of your introduction should mention the two reasons why you liked the book. That's your thesis statement, your main idea.
3. The next paragraph will be your summary. That will be followed by your two paragraphs on the reasons you liked the book.
4. Your last paragraph is your conclusion. Restate your reasons for liking the book — in a new way! Don't use the same sentence as before. Say whether or not you recommend the book and who you recommend it to. Write your final sentence with the word "I" in it. What is your final thought on the book?

Day 77

1. Turn to Day 61 in your workbook and think about what makes writing good or bad. Do you need to change anything to make your writing better?
   - Yes! No matter how well you wrote it, something can be improved.
2. Assemble all of the paragraphs for your book review together if you haven't already.
3. Think about how you could make better word choices or make longer sentences.
4. Read your book review out loud. Listen for trouble spots where it doesn't sound right or makes you stumble. Fix them.
5. Take your time and make it right. This is all you have to do today.
6. When you think your book review is great, add your name and date in the top right corner and a title to the top middle of the page.
7. Print it out and give it to your parents to include in your portfolio.

Day 78

1. You discover a bottle that says "Drink me." Write a short story about your discovery, what you do, and what happens next. There's a page in your workbook for this.
2. This is a creative writing exercise. Be creative.

Day 79

1. Do you know when to use -er and -est and more and most? Adjectives that are used to compare two things are called comparative adjectives. There are a few guidelines for changing an adjective into a comparative adjective.
   - If the adjective has one syllable, simply add –er to the end to make it comparative. If the word is a consonant-vowel-consonant word, you need to double the ending consonant before adding –er. If the word ends in e, simply add –r.
     - big dog   smart kid   brave hero
     - bigger dog   smarter kid   braver hero

   - If the adjective ends in y, change the y to an i before adding –er.
     - happy baby   silly clown
     - happier baby   sillier clown

   - For many adjectives with more than one syllable, simply add "more" to the regular adjective to make the comparative form.
     - colorful sunset   intelligent design
     - more colorful sunset   more intelligent design

   - And of course, there are many words that just don't follow a rule.
     - far walk, farther walk   little time, less time
     - bad cold, worse cold   good show, better show

2. Complete the worksheet and then check your answers. Did you spell them correctly?

Day 80

1. Your worksheet has a spelling activity and a grammar activity.
2. The spelling activity is to just find words in the jumble. There is an example to show you how to get started.
3. The verb section is asking if a word is a main verb, a helping verb, or a contraction.
   - Contractions are easy because they have an apostrophe. I <u>don't</u> see how you'd miss it.
   - In #3 above IS is the helping verb. It's helping the main verb, ASKING.

Day 81

1. You are basically working on spelling today. The first part of your worksheet today is on recognizing the correct homophone. Remember: homophones are when words sound alike but are spelled differently.
   - Its and it's are homophones. An apostrophe shows that one is a contraction of two words. "It's" means it is.
   - Other homophones aren't that easy to tell apart. You have to just know which is which. Trust yourself on what looks write. Did you catch that? I used the wrong homophone. It should be, "On what looks right."
2. The second part of the page is a word search.
   - Words go left to right, top to bottom, and diagonal following those same directions. There is one exception.

Day 82

1. In your workbook write a short story using a pair of homophones. (See Day 81 if you need a reminder.)
2. Make sure they are spelled correctly!
3. Get a hug and/or high five if you use more than one set.

Day 83

1. "If everybody minded their own business…the world would go around a great deal faster than it does." (From *Alice in Wonderland*) Another character disagrees with the woman who says this.
2. What do you think? Should people mind their own business or not? Which is better and why?
3. Answer in your workbook in complete sentences. You should always begin by restating the question. I think people should (or shouldn't) mind their own business because…

Day 84

1. Your worksheet today is on possessives.
   - A possessive shows that something belongs to someone. You add an apostrophe S unless there is already an S there. (Sometimes people will add an extra S when the word is pronounced with an extra S, such as Jones's.)

- It is Michael's bike.
- It is Michelle's bike.
- It is their family's bike.
- It is the children's bike
- It is the kids' bike.
- It is the Billings' bike.
- It is Chris' bike. It's Chris's bike. (I don't personally use the extra S, but it can be accepted as okay.)
- You don't use an apostrophe to make something plural, for the most part.
  - There have been many Fourth of July's is incorrect.
  - Occasionally, you can break the rule if you need to. Sometimes I write lessons about the alphabet and I have to write about <u>as</u>, as in A's. It's much clearer if I write it "incorrectly."

Day 85

1. Write about what you think makes a good leader. Is a good leader like a queen who rules with threats? What qualities make a good leader and why? How would those qualities affect those they lead?
2. Answer in your workbook with complete sentences. Remember to begin by restating the question. A good leader is…

Day 86

1. There is a spelling activity on your page, an unscramble. There are definitions to help you try to figure out the words. The first ones are short to help you get started.
2. The second part of the page is a simple conjunctions exercise mostly to help you realize there are different kinds of conjunctions besides and, or, but.

Day 87

1. Read this list of compare and contrast transition words. You will need some of these words in your next writing assignment. There are, of course, other words and phrases you can use, but you should use some transition words in your comparing and contrasting that you will be doing.
   - likewise, similarly, in the same way, in like manner, in a similar fashion
   - however, though, otherwise, on the contrary, in contrast, at the same time
2. You are going to start writing a compare and contrast essay. You will compare (tell how they are the same) and contrast (tell how they are different) the last two novels you have read. I will use these books as an example: *Treasure Seekers* and *Alice's Adventures in Wonderland*.
3. On your worksheet today, list things that are the ***same*** about the books. In my example they were both written in the last half of the 19th century and they were both written by English authors. Those might not be important to your essay, but we're not thinking about that now. You are just trying to think of as many things as possible of how they are similar. Think of any ways the characters, setting, plot, etc. are similar. There are some questions on the page to get you started.

Day 88

1. Use your workbook page for today to write ideas for what's *different* about the two books. One thing to do is to look at your list from Day 87 of how they are the same and think about when they stopped being the same.
2. From my example:
   - They both have a child for the main character, *but* the one book has four children.
   - They both start at a family home, *but* the one leaves reality and goes to a **surrealistic** land.
   - They both have adventures, *but*…
   - They both are trying to solve problems, *but*…
3. Today you are brainstorming for the contrasting part of your essay.

Day 89

1. You are going to write your thesis statement today, the point your essay is going to make.
2. FIRST, you need to decide on three different things that you can compare and contrast in your essay–ways they are the same and ways they are different. You can use my examples or your own. Use your lists for ideas.
   - The differences and similarities in settings and characters.
   - The differences and similarities in their adventures.
   - The differences and similarities in how their problems were solved.
3. Write your thesis statement, your main point. This will be your last sentence in your first paragraph. It should mention the three things that you will compare and contrast in your essay.
4. There is no worksheet for today. I recommend typing it and typing this essay. We'll be working on it over several days.

Day 90

1. Write your introduction. Start with an interesting sentence–a quote, a question, a comment. Then introduce each book in a sentence or two. Then comes your thesis statement which you have already written.
2. On Day 89 you decided on three things to compare and contrast in your essay. For each one, write at least one way the books are similar and at least one way the books are different.
   - This isn't part of your essay, just preparing for the next part of your essay.

Day 91

1. Write one of your three middle paragraphs. Those three paragraphs are called the body of your essay.
2. The first paragraph of the body should be about the topic you listed first in your thesis statement.

3. The first sentence in the paragraph is the topic sentence for that paragraph. It's your introduction for the paragraph and will tell what point you are going to make in that paragraph.
4. Then comes the body of the paragraph. In this part you will include your examples.
5. Then comes the conclusion of your paragraph. This sums up your point.

Day 92

1. Write one of your three middle paragraphs. Those three paragraphs are called the body of your essay.
2. The second paragraph of the body should be about the topic you listed second in your thesis statement.
3. The first sentence in the paragraph is the topic sentence for that paragraph. It's your introduction for the paragraph and will tell what point you are going to make in that paragraph.
4. Then comes the body of the paragraph. In this part you will include your examples.
5. Then comes the conclusion of your paragraph. This sums up your point.

Day 93

1. Write one of your three middle paragraphs. Those three paragraphs are called the body of your essay.
2. The third paragraph of the body should be about the third topic you listed first in your thesis statement.
3. The first sentence in the paragraph is the topic sentence for that paragraph. It's your introduction for the paragraph and will tell what point you are going to make in that paragraph.
4. Then comes the body of the paragraph. In this part you will include your examples.
5. Then comes the conclusion of your paragraph. This sums up your point.

Day 94

1. There is a capitalization practice on your worksheet today.
2. Here's a reminder of what is capitalized.
   - Names: names of places, names of people, names of things
     - We don't capitalize little words in the middle of names, but we do capitalize them in the beginning of names.
       - *John the Baptist, The Great Mouse Detective, The Grapes of Wrath, Of Mice and Men*
     - It gets a little tricky. The president isn't capitalized. It's a job. But, when he is addressed as President, when he is being spoken to, then it's his name at the moment, and it is capitalized.
     - We travel east, but in the East there are many spices. The one is a direction. The other is the name of a location.
   - In quotations we capitalize the first letter of the quote. If it's an interrupted quote and continues after a speech tag, then the first letter after the quotation mark isn't

capitalized in the second half because it's the middle of a sentence being continued from the first part of the quote.

- In a letter we capitalize the opening: Dear John and the closing: Yours Truly.

3. When you finish with your worksheet, you are going to write your conclusion.
4. The first sentence of your conclusion restates your thesis. Don't use the same sentence though!
5. Add something new.
6. End with a comment that sums up your thoughts on the books.

Day 95

1. Look again at the list of compare and contrast transition words. Do you use any of those? Would they help you write better sentences? Add at least one of those words or phrases into your essay.
    - likewise, similarly, in the same way, in like manner, in a similar fashion
    - however, though, otherwise, on the contrary, in contrast, at the same time
2. Read your essay out loud. Change anything that doesn't sound right.
3. Use the checklist in your workbook for today to see what needs improving.
4. Fix your essay. Make it right.
5. When you are pleased, print it out. Save it.

Day 96

1. You are going to be finding correctly capitalized sentences again. Refer to Day 94 if you want to refresh yourself on the rules.
2. Today in your workbook you are also going to practice spelling plurals. Here are your spelling rules for when you say there are many.
    - If it ends with an F or an FE, then the F is changed into a V and the plural ends in ES.
        - wife – wives
    - If it ends with an O, add an ES.
        - tomato – tomatoes
    - If it ends with an ON, change it to an A.
        - phenomenon – phenomena
    - If it ends with an IS, change it to an ES.
        - thesis – theses
    - If it ends with a US, change it to an I.
        - focus – foci
    - Most are given an S.
    - Those ending in S, SH, CH, X, Z are given an ES.
    - Words that end in a consonant and then Y are changed from Y to I and ES is added.

Day 97

1. On your worksheet you'll be working with those same spelling rules. Look at Day 96 if you need help remembering any of them.
2. Today you are going to practice comma rules.
   - Commas go between items in a list.
   - Commas go between date words and numbers.
   - Commas go before the conjunction in a compound sentence.
   - Commas go after the introduction to a sentence if it's followed by a complete sentence.
   - Commas go around extra, unnecessary information.
3. Do your best to put in the missing commas on the page.

Day 98

1. Today's worksheet is on irregular verbs. I can't give you a list of rules because they don't follow a pattern. They are irregular.
2. Normally you add an ED to make a verb past tense. These are irregular verbs, so they don't follow that pattern.
3. There is also more than one form of the past tense.
   - We drove all night to get there. We had driven all night, so we were really tired.
   - I was tired. I had been tired all day.
   - I drank the milk. I had drunk the last of the milk.
4. Even though it seems tricky, it's easy if you grew up listening to correct standard English grammar. Only one answer will sound correct. It's important to your writing that you use standard grammar in your everyday life and to speak with people who use proper grammar. It's the way to know what's right when things like this don't follow the rules. Reading good books will also keep proper grammar in mind.

Day 99

1. Today's worksheet is like Day 98's. Take a look at those directions if you want a reminder about past tense verb choice.

Day 100

1. The main way we show possession is by adding an apostrophe S. If there is already an S at the end of the word, then for the most part we just put an apostrophe on the end of it.
2. There are possessive pronouns as well.
   - That is my book. It is mine.
   - That is your book. It is yours.
   - That is his book. It is his. (or her/hers or its)
   - That is our book. It is ours.
   - That is their book. It is theirs.
   - There are no apostrophes in possessive pronouns.
3. Your task today in your workbook is to insert the apostrophe. The Ss are already there.

Day 101

1. *There were several others on the walls, but the boy thought there must be something peculiar about this one, for it had a graceful frame of moss and cones about it, and on a little bracket underneath stood a vase of wild flowers freshly gathered from the spring woods.* (p. 48, *Little Men)*
2. Let's write a sentence like this one in the section provided at the bottom of your worksheet.
    *   *There were several others on the walls.* That could be a sentence all by itself. The subject is SEVERAL OTHERS ON THE WALLS. There is a predicate (the rest of the sentence containing the verb): THERE WERE
    *   Usually subjects come first, but not always.
    *   Write a sentence.
    *   My example: I <u>ran home</u>.
    *   What is the subject and <u>predicate</u> of your sentence. (Hint: EVERY word is either part of the subject or part of the predicate.)
3. Now let's look at the next part of the sentence.
    *   *but the boy thought there must be something peculiar about this one*
    *   Without the BUT at the beginning, this could also be a sentence. The subject is THE BOY. The predicate is THOUGHT THERE MUST BE SOMETHING PECULIAR ABOUT THIS ONE
    *   The BUT is a conjunction.
    *   If we use a conjunction and are following it with what could be a complete sentence, then we use a comma before the conjunction.
    *   Take your sentence from before. Replace the period with a comma. Write a conjunction. Add another subject and predicate.
    *   My example: I <u>ran home</u>, but the front door <u>was locked</u>.
    *   What is the conjunction, subject, and <u>predicate</u> of the new part of your sentence?
4. Now, let's move on.
    *   Next, we find another comma and the word "for." That's considered a conjunction, so we should find a subject and predicate in the next part of the sentence.
    *   *for it had a graceful frame of moss and cones about it* What is the subject? What is the predicate?
    *   Now you write. Take your sentence and change the period into a comma, add a conjunction (and, or, but, so, for, yet, nor). Then add another subject and predicate.
    *   Here's my example: I <u>ran home</u>, but the front door <u>was locked</u>, nor <u>was</u> the back door <u>unlocked</u>.
    *   What is the subject and <u>predicate</u> you added?
    *   If the subject and predicate of my new part confuses you, read it as a question, "Was the backdoor unlocked?" That makes sense, right? A question is a type of sentence, so you can see that my new part has everything a sentence needs.
5. Last part…
    *   *and on a little bracket underneath stood a vase of wild flowers freshly gathered from the spring woods.*
    *   What is AND? Could this part of the sentence be a sentence on its own? If so, it has a subject and predicate. What is the subject? What is the predicate? Pay attention. The subject "does" the verb. What's the verb and what's doing that?

- Now finish your sentence. You'll need another comma because you are using a conjunction and what could be its own sentence.
- Take your sentence. Change the period into a comma. Add a conjunction and a subject and predicate.
- Read your sentence to an audience.
- Here's my example: I <u>ran home</u>, but the front door <u>was locked</u>, nor <u>was</u> the backdoor <u>unlocked</u>, but I <u>found my way inside through a hole in the porch screen</u>.
- It's not complicated to write long sentences once you see how they are put together. I expect your sentences to grow!

6. Unscramble the words. Do your best. They are vocabulary from *Little Men*.

Answers #4   Subject: it
Predicate: had a graceful frame of moss and cones about it
#5   *and* is a conjunction.
Subject: *a vase of wild flowers freshly gathered from the spring woods*
Predicate: *on a little bracket underneath stood*

Day 102

1. You are going to test yourself on punctuation today. Do you remember that commas go before the quotation marks, between items in a list, between date numbers and date words, before a conjunction in a compound sentence, after an introductory phrase or dependent clause that opens a sentence, and to separate out unnecessary information?
2. You will also be checking for capitalization, ending punctuation, and apostrophes. Apostrophes are used in contractions, where two words are combined, and to show possession.
3. Pay attention and take your time to make sure you find all the mistakes on the worksheet. You are playing editor today.

Day 103

1. *The **sun** <u>shone</u> in as if he enjoyed the fun, the little **stove** <u>roared</u> beautifully, the **kettle** <u>steamed</u>, the new **tins** <u>sparkled</u> on the walls, the pretty **china** <u>stood</u> in tempting rows, and **it** <u>was</u> altogether as cheery and complete a kitchen as any child could desire.* (*Little Men* p. 72) (I marked the **simple subject** and <u>simple predicate</u> in each part–that means just the noun and verb from the subject and predicate.)
2. What mood/feeling does the sentence produce?
3. These commas are followed by subjects and predicates but not conjunctions. Why are there commas then?
4. Write a list of things where each contains subjects and predicates. My example is below. There's a spot for this on your worksheet for today.
   - My example: On our street there are boys playing soccer, a bulldozer digging, a postman making his rounds, and pigeons watching it all.
5. The rest of your worksheet is about word choice, using the correct pronoun or the correct verb tense.

Answers #2   It gives a happy, playful feeling.
#3   It is a list. You use commas to separate things in a list. There is an "and" before the last item in the list.

Day 104

1. You are editing again today.
   - Look for misspelled words, especially incorrectly used homophones, where words sound the same but are spelled differently.
   - Check for commas, ending punctuation, and capitalization.
   - Apart from the beginning of sentences, which includes the first word of a quote, you capitalize names. Most of the time that's clear, but sometimes it's not. The sentences below use the same word (or similar word) in lowercase and uppercase.
     - That's your mom, but when you call for her, you say Mom, because that's her name to you.
     - You are going to your grandfather's house, but you call him Grandpa.
     - At the park you might meet the ranger, Ranger Bob.
     - To figure out if you should capitalize words like this, think about if you could substitute it with a name. For instance, we're going to our grandpa's house. You wouldn't say, "We're going to our Lee's house." You could say, "We're going to Lee's house," or, "We're going to Grandpa's house." In that last case, it can be substituted with a name, so it is capitalized.
2. Complete your worksheet with careful attention. Don't miss anything!

Day 105

1. Choose a character from a book you are reading for school or one you finished recently. In your workbook write a paragraph about ways you are like that character and ways you are unlike that character.
   - Your first sentence is your introduction. For instance: There are a few ways I'm like _____, but there are many ways we are different.
   - Then you give examples from the book of what the character is like and tell how you are like that or not like that.
   - Then write your concluding sentence. For instance: I think that… I hope that…

Day 106

1. Today in your workbook you are correcting misspelled words. Can you spot them? Remember to think about the correct spelling of homophones.

Day 107

1. A preposition is a relational word. It tells the relationship of a noun or pronoun to another part of the sentence. That sounds strange; it will be easier to give you some examples.
   - I'm taking the book with me.
     - With is the preposition.
     - Me is the pronoun.
     - It's telling the relationship between me and the book. It's telling where the book is.

- Prepositions are mostly locational words. They tell about something's location.
  - I put the book under the table.
    - Under is the preposition.
    - The table is the noun.
    - The preposition is telling the relationship between the table and the book. It's giving the location of the book in connection with the table.

2. You use these all the time, and they are *always* used along with a noun or pronoun. Together, they are called a prepositional phrase. All prepositions are in prepositional phrases. Every prepositional phrase begins with a preposition.
   - at the end
   - after work
   - before dinner
   - behind the couch
   - beside the blue car
   - around the corner
   - up the tallest tree
   - during lunch
   - in Memorial Park
   - from me

3. Take a book. Place it in as many different places that you can think of and tell the prepositional phrase that describes where it is. (eg. Near the door, with the paper…)
   - Those are all prepositional phrases. The first word you are saying is the preposition.

4. When these words are found in places other than in prepositional phrases, then they are not prepositions.
   - Look up in the sky.
     - Up is not a preposition. It's with the verb, look, not with the noun, sky. In the sky is the prepositional phrase.
   - Come around after lunch.
     - Around is not a preposition. It's with the verb, not with the noun, lunch. After lunch is the prepositional phrase.
   - Up and around in these cases are adverbs since they are with the verb. They are describing how to do the verb. That's an adverb's job.

5. On the worksheet today you are identifying prepositions.

Day 108

1. Write a few sentences about an imaginative game that you and your friends have played. There is a place on your worksheet for this.
2. Then you are also going to read the story on the page and underline all of the prepositions. I found 13. Can you find them all? It's not silly <u>of</u> me to think you can! Hmm…why did I just underline OF?

Day 109

1. Write a few sentences about a time that you apologized to someone for spoiling their fun and tried to make him/her happy again. There's a place on the worksheet for that.
2. On your worksheet today you are going to be identifying parts of a sentence. They each have a subject, a predicate, and a prepositional phrase. Follow the directions on the page and take a look at the example before you begin.
   - Remember that the preposition is always the first word in a prepositional phrase. I listed some prepositional phrases for you on Day 107 if you want to go back and read that list as a reminder.
   - The subject is what the sentence is about and the predicate is everything else.
   - If sentences with a question confuse you, then think about them as declarative sentences. Are you finished with that? You are finished with that.

Day 110

1. Write a story in your workbook describing going somewhere and how you got there.
2. Use at least ten prepositional phrases.

Day 111

1. In your workbook, write about a time when you wanted to "be good" or improve some weakness in
   your character. Did you ask God to help you?

Day 112

1. Do you remember what prepositions are?
   - Think about a book and table. What is the relationship of the book to the table?
     - <u>under</u> the table
     - <u>on</u> the table
     - away <u>from</u> the table
     - <u>beside</u> the table
     - part <u>of</u> the table
     - <u>next</u> to the table
     - <u>with</u> the table
     - <u>about</u> the table
     - …
   - Those are each prepositional phrases. Each prepositional phrase begins with a preposition. Those are underlined. The table is the **object of the preposition**. An object is always a noun or pronoun.
2. "Over the river and through the woods to grandmother's house we go…" Do you know that song? What are the prepositional phrases in what I wrote? What are the prepositions? What are the objects of the prepositions?
3. In your workbook is a quiz about prepositions and their objects.

Answers #2: Prepositions: over, through, to; Prepositional phrases: over the river, through the woods, to grandmother's house; Objects of the prepositions: river, woods, house

Day 113

1. Your worksheet today is on finding and identifying prepositions.

Day 114

1. Write a nursery rhyme in your workbook. Need an idea? Make it about huckleberries.
2. Take note: rhymes rhyme.

Day 115

1. Today you will be practicing the word there, and they're, and their. They're moving their car over there.
   - Remember that a contraction is two words put together. "They're" is really they are.
   - Their is the possessive pronoun. It belongs to them.
   - There is an adverb. It tells about how they are moving their car. They are moving it there.
2. There is also a little spelling activity on the page.

Day 116

1. Today in your workbook you just have to find the prepositional phrases.

Day 117

1. This is easy peasy today. Prepositional phrases begin with prepositions and end with the object of the preposition. You'll be finding both today in your workbook.
2. You can give this to a parent to add to your portfolio.

Day 118

1. Today in your workbook you are going to be filling in the object of the preposition as a pronoun. To do that, you have to use the object pronoun.
   - behind ME, with US, toward HIM   (not behind I, with we, toward he — those sound weird, right?)

Day 119

1. When you write using the word I, you are using what's called the first person.
   - Can you find a book in your house where the story is told in the first person?

2. It's easier to find books written in the third person. That's when the story is about he or she or them. The author is telling the story like they are watching it, not participating in it.
3. You will be identifying adverbs and prepositions today in your workbook.
4. Two things to remember:
    - Good is an adjective. Well is an adverb. You do something well and the result is good.
    - We don't use double negatives. There is not any here. Never, there is not none here. Not and none are both negative. They don't belong next to each other.

Day 120

1. Write a fractured fairy tale. That means, take a famous fairy tale story and make your own version of it.
2. Here are your directions.
    - Choose a fairy tale.
    - Read it if you need a refresher.
    - Then write the story from another point of view.
    - Choose a character to be "I" in the story. For instance, in the *Three Little Pigs* you could write it from the wolf's point of view. He could be the "I" and tell the story from his perspective.
    - You could give this to a parent to add to your portfolio. You might want to consider typing this one, but there is a page for it in your workbook.

Day 121

1. You are going to be finding the correct place for the apostrophe today in your workbook. Here are some reminders and maybe a new thing or two.
    - Plurals aren't made with apostrophes. Plural means more than one. Apostrophes show possession.
    - To show possession write an apostrophe and the letter S after the word. If it ends in S, just add an apostrophe.
        - Make sure your apostrophe goes after the word, whether singular or plural. If there are many boys playing a game, it's the boys' game, not the boy's game. The second shows possession by one boy. The first shows that the game belongs to many boys.
    - Possessive adjectives don't need an apostrophe: yours, ours, its.
    - Here's what to do when there is more than one person possessing something. If the something belongs to both of them together, then add an apostrophe to only the second name mentioned. If they each own the thing, they each get an apostrophe.
        - Ted and Bill's adventure is exciting. They are having an adventure together.
        - John's and Bill's hands are filthy. They both have dirty hands.

Day 122

1. In your workbook there is a parts-of-speech activity. I'll let you try it on your own. Flip back in the book if you have trouble remembering what any of the parts of speech are. Do your best and learn from any mistakes. Every mistake is an opportunity to learn. Don't miss your opportunities.
2. Today you will also be practicing speaking. Read this poem aloud and finish the last line. It should rhyme! Read the poem with rhythm. Pause after lines and stanzas. (The poem is from *Little Men*, chapter 17.)

> I write about the butterfly,
> It is a pretty thing;
> And flies about like the birds,
> But it does not sing.
>
> First it is a little grub,
> And then it is a nice yellow cocoon,
> And then the butterfly
> Eats its way out soon.
>
> They live on dew and honey,
> They do not have any hive,
> They do not sting like wasps, and bees, and hornets,
> And to be as good as they are we should strive.
>
> I should like to be a beautiful butterfly,
> All yellow, and blue, and green, and red;
> But I should not like to . . .

Day 123

1. Write feedback to the author of the paragraph on your workbook page. You can use the editing checklist on Day 45 for reminders.
2. Mark any corrections in spelling or grammar. Then write a note to the author. Tell what was good about the paragraph. Then offer specific feedback for how to improve it.

Day 124

1. You will be identifying parts of speech today in your workbook.
2. Prepositions are location words, telling where something is in relation to something else.
3. Find the prepositions in each set of four groups of words, and then write in the part of speech for the second section.
   - Don't be thrown off by the Did You Know? box. You won't be using all those parts of speech. Those aren't directions.

Day 125

1. Write a letter to a friend or family member.
2. Pay attention to the capitalization and punctuation of the letter.
   - Capitalize your greeting words and your closing words. Both the greeting and closing are followed by a comma.
     - Dear Mom,
     - Love,
3. There is a page in the workbook, but if you want to send your letter, write it on a different piece of paper!

Day 126

1. Today in your workbook you are practicing with a pair of confusing words.
2. When you lose something, it's lost.
3. When something is loose, it's not tight.
   - You can picture that the second one is not tight; it's more spread out with two O's instead of one.

Day 127

1. Complete the word search in your workbook to practice your spelling.

Day 128

1. Practice your parts of speech today in your workbook.

Day 129

1. Today there is a simple activity in your workbook focusing on summarizing.
2. Choose the best summary and then write your own.

Day 130

1. Today in your workbook, you are going to practice with another confusing pair of words.
2. Who's is a contraction that is short for who is.
3. Whose is a possessive that is asking to whom something belongs.

Day 131

1. On your workbook page for today, describe the main character of a story you've recently read for school.
2. If this character were to be bullied, how would he respond? If this character was in a spelling bee, would she win or run away with stage fright? What do you think? You are going to be writing a short story. You need to know your character so well that you would know how he would react in any situation.

3. Here's a reminder about what to think about when writing.
   - Ideas—the main message
   - Organization—the internal structure of the piece
   - Voice—the personal tone and flavor of the author's message
   - Word Choice—the vocabulary a writer chooses to convey meaning
   - Sentence Fluency—the rhythm and flow of the language
   - Conventions—the mechanical correctness
   - Presentation—how the writing actually looks on the page
     - From http://educationnorthwest.org/traits/trait-definitions

Day 132

1. Read the beginning of the first chapter of *What I Learned Over Summer Vacation.*
2. On your workbook page, describe the character's "voice." What's the tone? Is it serious? Informal? Funny? Conversational? Can you hear the "I" character talking in your head? What does the main character sound like?
3. What are some things you think this character would say? What are some things this character would never say?

Balderdash

School started back this week, and my teacher said we each had to take a turn telling the class what we did over the summer. Sarah and Michael, the twins, told all about their trip to space camp. They're practically astronauts already. Randy told about skiing in Chile in July! I've never even been skiing in January. Julie flew in a hot air balloon, and Steve built a car, though I'm pretty sure his dad did most of the work. Their summers were all so exciting, so interesting, so unique, that I knew my summer vacation story had to be absolutely amazing. I wanted them to fall out of their seats for the sheer thrill of it! Do you want to hear my story? You might want to strap on a seat belt.

Summer started out in the usual way with a bus ride home. I'm the first one on and the last one off, so it was just me and bus driver Fran left on the bus when a hail storm ripped through the sky like my big brother opening a box of marshmallow cereal. The hail stones were so big that they tore right through the bus hood and crushed the engine. Well, the bus wouldn't go anywhere without an engine, but I got an idea. The hail was covering the road like marbles. I took off a bus tire and told bus driver Fran I could get myself home. I laid the tire down flat and sat in it like a sled. I shoved off and used my backpack as a paddle both to steer and to push my way along the rolling, marbley hailstones, and I started slipping and sledding down the road.

That worked for a while until I started slipping and sledding down a big hill and lost grip of my paddle-backpack. I was careening down the steep hill, screaming at the top of my lungs and instead of trying to steer, I wrapped my arms around my face. I didn't stop screaming when I realized the ground wasn't underneath me anymore. I didn't even stop screaming when I felt myself splash down. I stopped screaming when my tire hit a big rock and spilled me into the water. That's when I realized I was drifting down a river.

Sputtering and spitting the water spurting into my mouth, I grabbed hold of something floating along with me and just focused on staying afloat. I was looking around me and just saw trees on both sides, and I was wishing I knew my geography because then maybe I would know where I was being carried. But then instead of worrying, I reminded myself I was on summer vacation and getting wet is a big part of summer vacation, so I figured I was getting off to a great start!

The water current slowed down and the river turned into a creek, and I found myself lying on the back of a baby elephant. I know you are thinking, what! Where did that elephant come from? I know that's what you are thinking because that's what I was thinking. I realized that the thing I grabbed hold of that was floating down the river was a baby elephant's trunk, not a branch or something. As the river thinned out, she rose up out of the water and took me with her.

This, of course, was an unexpected turn of events and required some quick thinking on my part. Unfortunately, in the last 180 days of school no one taught us anything about communicating with or controlling elephants, so I did my thinking while letting her carry me wherever she wanted to go. I had, however, read books and seen movies about animals who eventually found their way home, so I decided to trust that she was headed for her home, which I figured was probably the zoo since, how many people do you know have a baby elephant for a pet? Exactly.

The zoo wasn't our first stop though. The creek was surrounded by trees and I found myself on an elephant ride through the woods. I heard a cackling sound, you know, a really loud laugh that's not exactly contagious like a friendly, funny laugh is supposed to be. Then I heard yelling. Then I heard a squeal. It actually made me feel better that I was with Bucko, that's what I named the elephant. It just came out, "Hey, Bucko, where you taking me?" Like that. Bucko didn't seem fazed by the noises that I pretended not to be fazed by.

It wasn't long before the other noises stopped, probably because the crunching of the elephant's stomping was noise enough for everyone. Finally, we came into a small clearing in the woods and found the source of the cackle, yell and squeal. There was a horse, but the horse hadn't made any of those sounds. He was decorated with bright red and blue ropes and blinders and didn't pay any attention at all to me and Bucko. The dog had been the source of the squeal, and he repeated his squealy show when the cackler grabbed hold of him and wouldn't let him sniff or chase or whatever dog instinct had come over him in the moment.

Day 133

1. Read the next part of the first chapter of *What I Learned Over Summer Vacation*.
2. Here's a quote from the Balderdash stories.
   - "Mrs. Carp came over with her tomatoes. That was just a ruse. She wanted a reason to come over to complain. No irony there."
3. Irony means that something is the opposite of what you would expect. Why is it <u>not</u> ironic that Mrs. Carp came over to complain. (Hint: look up the definition of carp.)
4. Want an example of something that is ironic? A fire station burning down is ironic. You wouldn't expect that to happen. Write an example of an ironic situation, something that's the opposite of what you would expect.

Answer #3 Carp means to complain. Her name literally means complain, so it was not unexpected for her to complain.

The yeller was a boy, small compared to me, not that I told you how tall I am, but he wasn't taller than me and he wasn't a baby or toddler or anything either. I don't know what he had yelled about, but now his face was stone still, a looked-like-he-wasn't-breathing kind of still.

The cackler did it again, a sort of laugh-cough baring a mouth with four teeth left in it. Her hair was black or dyed but most of it was covered with a scarf that rivaled the horse's decorations for brightness of color. She asked me how I came to be riding Apara (*say a like the word a, the word par, then the word a again*). I asked if Bucko's name was really Apara and she said it was. She said the elephant was named that because she comes and goes as she pleases. She said she's like an apparition; she's there one minute and gone the next. Turns out my boy, Bucko, was a girl.

I mostly sat silent, which is not how I usually sit, but she knew Bucko, Apara, and she was talking like she's known her her whole life, which was impossible because I was the one riding her down the river. I had to quickly explain the whole river thing, and she explained that Apara wasn't from the zoo but from the circus. In fact her son and daughter-in-law, yeller's parents, were part of the circus. They were acrobats and the mom could do a head stand on the head of the father all while riding on the back of Apara's mother.

I displayed my excitement at the thought of a perilous headstand and was promptly invited to see the circus in action when we returned Apara. This is the part where we get to know each other, and I find out they are Gypsies and had always traveled with the circus, as in my father's-father's-father-before-me-was-in-the-circus kind of always. The cackler started telling me the most amazing stories, stories of circuses, of runaway trains, of renegade elephants, of robbers in the woods. They were the most amazing, unique, exciting and interesting stories that had ever been told. Well, I don't know that for a fact, but by my subjective opinion, they were!

As I sat next to the Gypsy grandmother on a log by the fire with a pot of something cooking over it, I asked her how she came to live and tell such marvelous, stupendous, outrageous stories. She told me she was the best story teller because she had lived a lot of life and had learned the secret ingredient to telling a story.

I'm curious even if curiosity did kill the cat, but I'm not a cat, so I don't have to worry about that, and I asked her right away what the secret story ingredient was. She looked at me like she was scrutinizing my thoughts that I thought I had hidden. Then she cackled. I liked the cackle a lot more up close, with those four teeth waggling in front of me, than when I didn't know whose teeth that cackle was behind. Then she told me that she couldn't tell me the secret ingredient. "Not yet," she said. Oooo, now isn't that tantalizing? Not yet. I wasn't going to run home with a *not yet* promising that *some time* a secret would be revealed.

The cackler served me goolash. I don't know if that's really what it was, but that's what it looked like. That's what my dad calls dinner when he empties everything leftover in the fridge into a pot and adds water. They didn't have a fridge, but same idea. Then I saddled up on Bucko, or you could say climbed up onto Apara's back, and we followed the cackler and yeller riding in the cart pulled by the horse of many colors. Did you see us in our mini parade? You probably heard about it if you didn't. I love a parade and started waving at the gaping gawkers along our route to the circus. One little girl asked for my autograph. I obliged, of course.

While I was signing my Hancock, Apara started sniffing into the wind. As I handed back the paper to the little girl, Apara took off charging in a direction almost opposite of the horse and cart. I didn't have time to call for help. I just grabbed on and went for a wild ride. Apara galloped through the streets. People dove to the right and to the left to get out of the way. Cars crashed, distracted by the site of a rampaging pachyderm.

Apara ran as the crow flies and didn't seem to want to bother with dodging obstacles. They dodged her or they got run over. She crashed over the flower pots in front of the *Stop and Smell the Roses* flower shop. She crashed into the *Five and Ten* which has been indestructible for the last century. She managed to bulldoze her way through the aisles and out the loading doors in the back.

I managed to grab up a lollypop when we passed the front counter. I tossed a dollar from my pocket which I'm sure would cover the lollypop but certainly not the mess Apara made.

Day 134

1. Read the next part of the first chapter of *What I Learned Over Summer Vacation*.
2. Another writing trait is organization. Did the story "hook" you? Were you interested in reading from the first paragraph?
3. Also, when you get to the end of a story you should feel like the story is complete, that your questions have been answered, that the story has been wrapped up. Mostly endings make you feel very happy and satisfied. When you write, you want your stories to leave your audience feeling that way.

I popped the lollypop into my mouth and congratulated myself on snatching up a root beer flavored one. Apara wasn't slowing down, and I got to thinking about the circus acrobats, yeller's parents who rode on an elephant's back, his mother balancing upside-down on top of his father's head. I thought if they could do that, then I could probably ride standing up and sucking on a lollypop. I slowly got to my feet. I stood tall and threw my arms up in the air to signify my triumph. My left arm hit a traffic light post and knocked me off balance. I swung around the post and grabbed on with my lollypop still protruding from between my lips. I wrapped my legs tight around the pole and held on.

I didn't slide down right away because of the still-fresh memory of rope burn from gym class, but then I didn't dare slide down because two police dogs started barking at me and attacking the post as if that would somehow get me down. I went up. I made it all the way to the very top and sat on top of the traffic light. I guess my feet must have dangled down over the lights because cars starting stopping instead of going, but maybe they were just distracted from driving because a kid was sitting on the traffic light.

Traffic came to a standstill, as they say. The police came out of their office to see what the dogs were yapping at and what all the cars were honking at, and what they saw was me! I waved. They called in a helicopter. It circled overhead, and I had to climb up a rope ladder they dangled from the helicopter for me. But before they could take me home, they got a call about an elephant that had barreled into the annual peanut festival.

My synapses were firing and I figured it must be Apara at the peanut festival. I figured that must be how she got away from the circus in the first place and then away from me. She had smelled those peanuts and just couldn't control herself. She is just a kid after all. You may think there's no way she could smell that festival a full ten miles away, but elephants can actually smell twelve miles away. If you don't believe me, Google it. I'm telling the truth.

I felt like a spy, flying over town in a helicopter, looking for the trouble-making elephant. We spotted her easy. It's not like we were looking for a needle in a haystack. We were looking for an elephant in a peanut pile which had been a peanut pyramid before the peanut-loving pachyderm pounced on it. (Mr. Johnson always builds a peanut pyramid for the peanut festival.)

I pointed to Apara and looked over at the helicopter pilot to see if he could see her too, but the pilot wasn't looking down. He was looking awful. He was wriggling like he was trying to scratch an itch that covered his whole body and his lips were looking puffy. In fact his whole face was looking splotchy, red and bumpy. Then I remembered seeing something just like that before when my dad accidently ate some shellfish and we had to rush him to the hospital. It's easy to remember because I have a memento. My brother and I took pictures of ourselves wearing bedpans as hats.

I gestured to the helicopter pilot that his face was red and puffy and that he should let me down with the rope ladder to go get the elephant. I think he understood or at least was too puffy to care because he didn't object when I kicked the ladder out the helicopter door. He hovered over the peanut festival and I climbed down and jumped off onto a pile of plush peanuts, prizes for the pick-the-winning peanut game where you reach into a barrel and pick up a peanut, and if it has a mark on its shell you get a stuffed peanut, you know, like a stuffed animal but legume instead. I learned about legumes from my elderly neighbor.

Once I was on the ground, I had to formulate a plan. Apara was not going to want to leave her peanut paradise. I remembered that carrot-on-a-stick trick where you dangle a carrot in front of a horse to get him to go forward to try and get it. But I was smart enough to know it wouldn't work with Apara since her trunk could reach farther than my stick would. I walked around surveying the scene and taking an inventory of my assets. I learned how to do that from television. I was hoping something would inspire a brilliant plan to free the festival of their four-legged intruder.

Day 135

1. Read the end of the first chapter of *What I Learned Over Summer Vacation*.
2. Word choice is another writing trait. What are some words or phrases that make the story exciting and interesting?
3. What strong, exciting verb is used in this part of a sentence from the story?
   - "A hail storm ripped through the sky like my big brother opening a box of marshmallow cereal."
   - Why is this better than just saying it started to hail?
   - Does the simile make in image in your mind?
   Answer #3 ripped

Brilliance had yet to strike, so I got some cotton candy and sat for a spell. That's an expression. I didn't spell anything. I started listing my options. I could push or pull or pick her up. They all sounded really hard and somewhat painful. Then it hit me like a bolt of lightning, figuratively speaking. Wheels would make pushing and pulling easier, right? That thought inspired two words: bumper cars. And air holds up planes, why not an elephant? That thought inspired one word: parachute. Can you figure out what my plan was?

I politely borrowed the canopy that Apara had partially knocked down anyway from the peanut pyramid pavilion. I tied the four corners onto the poles of three bumper cars. I made a trail of peanuts from Apara into the two back cars. She climbed in and stood with her two front feet in the one car and her two back feet in the other. I opened the door to the exit and then climbed into the first car. I stepped on the gas, which is an expression too, especially since it's an electric car and doesn't have any gas in it. I hurled my car toward the exit and pulled Apara behind me. I would have loved to have seen the look on her face, but I'm a serious driver and kept my eye on the road, which is another figure of speech. I wasn't on the street but in the middle of the peanut festival.

Just as I had hoped, we had built up enough momentum (I learned that word in school) that we made it to the hill and started rolling down toward the moon bounce. One bump later and we were airborne. We landed on the air-filled castle and bounced up high. The parachute caught us and I demonstrated to Apara how to blow hot air into our parachute. She started blowing through her trunk, sending hot air into the parachute, and it lifted us up. I knew that hot air rises. I learned that from my dad when I complained about how hot my bedroom was.

So there we were, flying. We had made it over the fence when lightning struck, literally, that wasn't an expression. The hail storm must have been following me because it found me again. The hail knocked down our parachute and us with it. The metal rods on the back of the bumper cars must have looked pretty attractive to the lightening because it kept striking the one on the back of my car. I figure it must have had the highest pole. It was just what I needed. The electricity in the lightening powered up my car which propelled down the road at lightning speed, pun intended. My car was still tied onto Apara's cars, and the lightening was enough power for us all.

At first I forgot that I was supposed to be getting Apara to the circus. It was so cool getting to drive a car so fast and on a real road too, but it didn't take long before I realized I had to figure out where I was going, or I was going to crash. I started turning right and then left at each chance I got. I figured at least that way I wouldn't go in a circle. The sun was a bit behind me, so I figured I was heading eastish. I learned that the sun sets in the west from my grandfather. The problem was that it didn't mean anything to me that I was heading east.

I was going too fast to think too much. Then I saw my school, turns out that I had gone in a circle. I was back where I had begun my summer vacation. The storm blew on ahead of us and the lightening stopped and so did we without our energizer. We rolled into the school parking lot. It was empty. I guess students aren't the only ones eager to head home on summer vacation. I got out of my car and encouraged Apara out of hers. A new plan flashed into my brain. I discretely picked some flowers and gave them to Apara to hold with her trunk. With her nose thus occupied I climbed onto her back and tried my hand at directing her steps, using her ears as reigns. She got the message.

I knew my way home from school so that's where we went. I don't think I need to go into what my mother said when she saw me riding into the driveway on the back of an elephant. She's very understanding though, and once all of her questions were answered she escorted us to the circus. She drove slowly with her hazard lights flashing, and Apara and I followed.

At the circus we met the yeller and cackler and Apara's mom. I was invited to ride Apara in the show and my mom bought a ticket to watch. The circus was great, but I suspect the highlight was my riding Apara standing up while sucking on a lollypop.

After the circus ended and I was about to head home, the Gypsy grandmother pulled me aside and told me her secret ingredient that she added to every story to make it amazingly fascinating and wonderfully exciting and that's what I learned from the cackler – balderdash.

Balderdash
senseless talk or writing; nonsense

Day 136

1. " There was no way I was going to run away with the circus. That would be cliché and I'm full of surprises." (from one of the *Balderdash* stories)
2. Cliché refers to something that has been overused. "Run away with the circus" is the obvious, usual thing that's done in stories.
3. When you write your story, avoid clichés. Be unique!

4. The final writing traits are sentence fluency and proper use of grammar and punctuation. If you read the story out loud, does it flow smoothly? Does it sound nice or does it stumble and fall flat?

5. You are going to be writing a short story. There are two choices for the writing assignment. If you are using the EP Fifth Reader, you have read all the *Balderdash* stories; you could choose to write the next chapter in the book. Another option is to just write a fun short story.

6. Balderdash Assignment
    *   Write the next chapter story. The first step is deciding what new word the chapter will be called. Here are some ideas: imbrue, taint, soughing, punctilious, abate, oscillate, malodorous, intimation (Read this word carefully; it may not be what you think it is.)
    *   Look up the words and decide on your chapter title. Words have more than one definition. You can choose one if you like. You also need to pay attention to what part of speech your word is and make sure you use it that way. Start your chapter with the title and the definition. Decide how that word will be taught through your chapter story.
    *   When you are writing your story, see if you can throw in a vocabulary word from one of the other stories.
    *   Use the same character, voice, tone, word choice, etc. It should sound like it's from the same book.
    *   Remember not to be cliché; this character is full of surprises. Don't forget to throw in some balderdash!
    *   And, (I know I'm asking a lot) you should really try to add a "I learned that from…" sentence in your story. The character is always saying that. What else does the character use a lot? Idioms, expressions, figurative speech: "sat for a spell," "hit me like a bolt of lightning," "curiosity killed the cat," "all tied up in knots," "throw caution to the wind"…
    *   If you like your story, you can email it to me. I'm hoping to get a collection of these stories.

7. Short Story Assignment
    *   Today you will choose your character. Draw a picture or write a description. Your main character could be a person, an animal, a robot, whatever you decide.

8. Everyone:
    *   When you write your story, the main character is going to be the narrator. You will be writing in the first person, using "I." You will be writing in the first person. You aren't going to start writing today. On your worksheet make a list of ideas about what your character is like and what your character will do and say.

Day 137

1. Make a list of **plot events** on your worksheet for today. What's the character going to do first? Then what's going to happen? What will the character decide to do next? There should be at least three major plot events.

2. Today think about your **plot**. What are some things that the character could learn along the way? List a few ideas.

3. Here's a list of idioms. Have a list of at least five that you like and want to try to use if you can.
    - A dime a dozen
    - A drop in the bucket
    - A piece of cake
    - Up against the clock
    - Bite your tongue
    - Buy a lemon
    - Bend over backwards
    - Crack someone up
    - Down to the wire
    - Drive someone up the wall
    - Go for broke
    - Go out on a limb
    - Hit the sack
    - Hold your horses
    - Couldn't swing a cat
    - On the fence
    - Under the weather

Day 138

1. (EP Fifth Reader users: Work on your Balderdash writing assignment. Make sure the story shows the meaning of your word, and make sure you include your word in your story.)
2. Everyone: Start writing. Write a half of a page or more. Use your character's voice. You don't have to use dialogue. Let "I" tell the story. Write as the main character.
3. You'll be typing this one if you are able. There is no page in your workbook.

Day 139

1. Write. Write at least a half of a page.

Day 140

1. Today finish writing. If you just can't stop writing because it's so exciting, then you will just have to keep working on it when you have free time until you are done.
2. Read your story out loud to someone. Mark the spots that don't come out right.
3. Fix anything you found when reading it out loud.
4. Print it out. Save it.

Day 141

1. Here is one last grammar review before you work on your big writing project that you will edit to perfection with your ace grammar skills!
2. On your workbook page, read the questions first and then use the paragraph to find the answers.

Day 142

1. You are going to be writing a book. Yes, you! Writing a book can be fun! I've done it!
2. Today you are going to learn about **genres**.
3. Genres are types.
   - There are types of bread. They are all bread, but white bread and 12-grain whole wheat bread look different from each other and taste different from each other.
   - There are distinctions that make them different even though they are both bread.
4. Books come in **genres**. There are types of books. There are sad books and funny books, books about real people, books about fictional life in space.
5. You could write a mystery story or a fantasy story in a made-up world…There are many choices. You are going to be writing fiction, a made-up story. Here are some fiction genres to think about.
   - Fantasy – set in a made-up world
   - Historical fiction – made-up characters in a real historical setting
   - Humor – meant to entertain
   - Legend – based on a real person but doing made-up things
   - Mystery – solving a crime or figuring out secrets
   - Realistic fiction – true to life as if it could have happened
   - Science fiction – based on real or imagined science, often set in the future
   - Tall tale – funny story full of exaggerations
6. Your turn. Open a brand new word processing document. You can save it as "My Book" until you have a title. Write at the top of the page your genre.
7. Start thinking about your book, but we're not ready to start writing yet.

Day 143

1. When you write, you need to use specific nouns to make your writing more descriptive. What's the difference between these two sentences?
   - The man saw a dog as he crossed the road to get to the building.
   - Mr. Wong saw a poodle as he crossed the four-lane road to get to the bank.
     - The reader can't really picture what the author is thinking of if generic, broad nouns are used.
     - The second sentence is better in that the reader and the author are both picturing a poodle and a bank for instance.
2. Follow the directions on the worksheet to write specific nouns.
3. Make a list of six specific nouns that you might use in your book. Be specific. Don't write snake; write python (for example). Type these in your book document where you wrote your genre.

4. This list is for when you don't know what to write next. You can look at this list and find an idea for what to write next. I did this before I wrote my book and I put every one of them into my book. I got this idea from the *Little Blue School* blog. I used their ideas for how to write a book when I wrote my book, so I am using bits of those lessons here.

Day 144

1. Every story has a **protagonist**, the hero of the story. This will be your main character. That word is pronounced: pro-TAG-a-nist.
2. Fill out the worksheet about your main character.
   - Be as specific as possible. Does he have lots of friends? Do people think he's handsome? Is she loving towards her little sisters?
   - Who is this person? The better you know your character the better your story will be. You'll know just what he or she would do in a situation. Make sure your main character is not perfect. He or she needs at least one major flaw. She can't sing but she thinks she can. He can't whistle (and he'll need to in the story). She's painfully shy. He can't eat spaghetti. Whatever it is, it has to be part of the story.

Day 145

1. What adjectives would you use to describe your protagonist?
2. Adjectives help your readers picture just what you are picturing. If I wrote: I saw a dog. Each one of you would picture something different! If I wrote: I saw dog hairy enough that his eyes were concealed and large enough that he could lick my knee caps; I know because that's just what he was doing. Do you think we're picturing something more similar now? You need to describe what you are talking about. Specific nouns will help, so will adjectives.
   - On your worksheet today, you are going to write one adjective for every letter of the alphabet.
3. Do all that you can. At the end, when you can't think of any more and your brain is getting sore, then you can ask for help or get help online.

Day 146

1. Now your hero, your protagonist, needs a sidekick. Who is the best friend? It could be an animal.
2. Who is always there for the hero? Who is going to help your character accomplish their goals?
3. If you are using the EP Fifth Reader, Pollyanna's sidekick is her game! She keeps it with her at all times.
4. On your workbook page, describe this character just like you did your hero. Know everything about this character. Draw a picture.

Day 147

1. Now your story needs a villain, the **antagonist**, the bad guy.
   - Antagonist is pronounced, an-TAG-a-nist.
2. Your main character is out to do something and your antagonist is trying to stop him. He always gets in the way. (This doesn't *have* to be a person. In some books/movies it's the weather, for instance. The weather, technical difficulties, or "bad luck" keeps getting in the way of the main character accomplishing their goal.)
3. On your worksheet page, describe your villain. Know everything about your antagonist. Don't leave anything out. Your antagonist needs strengths and weaknesses. Any quirks or habits? Draw a picture.

Day 148

1. Now your antagonist needs a sidekick. Who is there to help carry out the tricky schemes?
2. On your worksheet for today, describe the character. Name, address, phone number…just kidding, unless you really want to, that's great! Know everything about this character. Draw a picture.

Day 149

1. Every story needs a **conflict**. Otherwise it will sound like this. He woke up. He went outside to play. He ate dinner. He went to bed. No excitement! Something needs to happen!
2. Earlier in the year you studied the parts of a story. In the story of Cinderella, the background that's part of the setting of the story is her losing her father. The incident that sets off the conflict is the announcement that the prince will choose a bride at the ball. Cinderella (protagonist) wants to go. The evil stepmother (antagonist) doesn't want her to. The conflict is set. The question is raised, "Will Cinderella marry the prince?"
3. What is your conflict? What does the hero try to do and the villian try to stop?
4. What incident will happen in the beginning of the book to set up the conflict and raise the question that will be answered at the end of the book?
5. Need ideas? Something is lost and needs to be found. Someone starts a journey. Something needs to happen to set the course for the whole rest of the book.
6. Use your worksheet for today to plan your conflict. What's the big question that needs answering? What is the antagonist going to try to do? What is the villain going to do about it? Write down the big question for the conflict and any ideas you have for what make take place in the conflict.

Day 150

1. You've practiced choosing specific nouns. How about verbs?
2. Write a specific verb for each of the verbs and adverbs on your worksheet today. Choosing more exciting words will make your book more exciting.
   - Instead of saying someone kept talking for a long time, you could they rambled.
   - Instead of saying that someone spoke unclearly, you could say they mumbled.

Day 151

1. Today you are going to describe the setting of your book. There will actually be many settings (specific rooms, places the character goes, etc.).
2. Here are some things to think about with setting:
   - Place (the castle, Chicago, the woods)
   - Location (the dining room, the top of the Sears tower, beside the old oak tree)
   - Objects (a vase of tulips, a pair of binoculars, a ring of mushrooms)
   - Time (morning, midnight, dusk)
   - Weather (stormy, clear sky, hot)
3. The time, weather, and maybe location will change throughout your novel. You need to make sure you let the reader know the setting of the chapter you are writing. If your novel takes place over a long time, the weather will need to change!
4. Today write a description of the overall setting of your book. On your worksheet you'll include
   - Time (today, 500 years ago, 500 years in the future)
   - General Location (in South Philadelphia, the Great Wall of China, in the Pacific Ocean, in space)
   - Specific Location (playground, store, apartment, castle, house, village, school, space station, planet–with specific name!)
   - Weather (what time of year is it, what is the weather generally)
5. Then draw a picture and write a description; add as many details as possible. Does it have an apple tree? A good climbing tree? A place to hide? A fence? A secret tunnel? How will this setting help or hinder the good guy? the bad guy?

Day 152

1. In your workbook, describe four different smaller settings in your book. They could be different places, different rooms, different buildings. Include as many details as possible.
2. List what objects are there. How could those objects help or hinder your characters? Think of how you could use them in your book.

Day 153

1. Do you know your basic story?
   - It's going to start with the background, setting the scene.
   - Then there's going to be an incident that sets off the conflict and asks the big question.
   - Then there is going to be conflict, complications, ups and downs.
   - Then there is the climax. This is the last big scene where we are about to find out the answer to the question. It's tense. We are in suspense.
   - Then there is the final scene where we find out what happens to everyone and everything is tied up neatly with a bow and we are satisfied and happy.
2. In your workbook write out each of those steps for your book. Add a few complications, conflict points, where your character seems to get ahead and then is knocked back down. In the beginning we think, "Of course, he's going to get there. Of course, he's going to

win." At some point we need to question, "Maybe he's not going to..." It needs to look bad for our main character.

Day 154

1. Let's think a little more about your story. There can be smaller stories within your story. Maybe the conflict is about winning the big game, but by the end, winning isn't as important anymore because he's made friends. Or maybe he's always fighting with his brothers, but in the story they need to work together to solve the conflict and they become friends. Maybe he's failing at school, but he discovers the secret formula needed to save the planet and gets an A+ in science.
2. Think about it. What would be the beginning, middle, and end for this smaller story? (for instance: fighting with brothers, working together, becoming friends)
3. Write your ideas on your workbook page.

Day 155

1. In your workbook, fill out the plot chart for a book or movie that you know really well.
2. Fill out the second chart for your book.

Day 156

1. Today you are going to fill out a chapter list.
2. Each chapter is its own little story. This is the chapter where he finds the ..... This is the chapter where he gets lost in... This is the chapter where he meets...
3. Your first chapter is your introduction, setting the background to the story.
4. By the end of that chapter or in the next chapter you should have your incident that will set off your question. Set your story in motion early!
5. Your last chapter is your resolution, what happens to everyone in the end.
6. The last few chapters before that is your climax, the exciting last event.
7. In between, your protagonist and antagonist each need to have times when they are ahead and when they are behind.
8. You may not be able to fill in all the chapter spots on the worksheet. That's okay. Do your best. Aim for ten.

Day 157

1. Today is the big day. You are going to start writing your novel. Aim at working on it for 30 minutes each day.
2. The most important thing is to write. Just write something. Momentum is very important to authors. Get on a roll. It's hardest to get the ball rolling. It's easier to keep it rolling. So just start writing. Write something.
3. You won't be working in your workbook anymore. If you are able to type your book, that would be easiest for editing.

Day 158

1. Write! Write! Write! Aim at working on it for 30 minutes each day.

Day 159

1. Write your book! Yeah!
2. Use all of the things we worked on together. Use all of your descriptions. Make sure to use your characters' strengths and weaknesses.

Day 160

1. Write! Make sure to describe your settings so that your audience is picturing what you are picturing.

Day 161

1. Write! Keep going! Don't stop!
2. When you write a dialogue, "hear" the people talking in your head. What do they sound like? How do they talk?

Day 162

1. Write! What object can you put in your story that will help out your character?

Day 163

1. Write! What's going to happen today?

Day 164

1. Write!

Day 165

1. **DON'T** Write!
2. Today, go back. Read your whole story from the beginning. It's best to read it out loud.
3. Is there anything you'd like to change?
4. Can you add more detail to your description of your characters or settings so that your audience pictures what you picture?
5. Can you picture your story as a movie in your mind?
6. Picture it as you read. Are there any gaps that you need to fill in?
7. Now, go back and read all of your answers from the days you described your characters and settings. Look at your answers when you wrote nouns and verbs.
8. Look at your chapter list and plot summary pages.
9. Are you happy with where you are? Fix anything you aren't happy with.

Day 166

1. Time to write again. Get going!

Day 167

1. Write! What problem is going to hinder your protagonist?

Day 168

1. Write!

Day 169

1. Write! If you are stuck, use an item from your list on Day 143.

Day 170

1. Write!

Day 171

1. Write!

Day 172

1. Write!

Day 173

1. Write!

Day 174

1. STOP!
2. Time to go back and read again.
3. Picture the movie of your story in your mind. Does it make sense? Fix anything that doesn't work right.
4. Think about your characters, settings, chapters, etc.
5. What haven't you added yet?
6. What needs to happen in your story?
7. Have you made conflict and complications for your protagonist?
8. What is going to happen next?
9. How are you going to get to your exciting climax?

Day 175

1. Write. Write lots and lots.

Day 176

1. Write. Write lots and lots.

Day 177

1. Write. Write lots and lots.

Day 178

1. Write. Write lots and lots.

Day 179

1. Write. Can you get to the end?

Day 180

1. You made it to the last day of school. I don't know where you are in your novel.
2. Keep writing if you have more to go.
3. If you got to the end, spend lots of time reading your novel and making it better.
4. Choose better words, change the lengths of your sentences. Add to your descriptions.
5. If you want to turn it into a real book, you can use a free service called CreateSpace. Follow their directions and you can publish your book for free. It will help you make a cover and everything. Then your friends and family can buy your book!

EP Language Arts 5

Workbook Answers

Day 2

Day 2: Spelling	Language Arts 5

How are your spelling skills? Use a vowel pair from the box to complete the words below. Vowel pairs can be used multiple times, and many words can take more than one vowel pair. (Some answers may vary)

eo	ai	ou	ea	ui	ee	oa	ua
ia	oe	oo	ie	oi	uo		

geode

p **eo** ple   g **ui** de   ch **ee** se

l **ea** ve   c **oa** t   h **ea** ven

qu **i** lt   g **ua** rd   l **oa** ves

q **uo** te   n **oi** se   th **ou** gh

th **ie** f   c **oo** ked   y **ou** th

fr **ie** nd   ch **ai** r   b **ea** uty

can **oe**   p **ia** no   d **ou** gh

Day 6

Day 6: Spelling • Parts of Speech	Language Arts 5

Pick the vowel pair that fills in the blank to correctly spell a word.

b **ea** t
oe   ea   ui   ua

l **ou** d
ee   oo   ou   oa

tr **ai** l
oi   oe   ai   eo

p **ee** l
ia   ie   uo   eo

d **ua** l
oo   oe   ua   ee

r **oa** d
ou   oe   ui   oa

Did you know? Some nouns can only be plural. *Jeans, scissors, heebie-jeebies, tweezers,* and *underpants* are a few examples of plurale tantum (Latin for "plural only") nouns.

Circle the part of speech that correctly labels the underlined word in each sentence.

Is anybody home?   noun   adverb   (pronoun)

The scientist used a microscope.   verb   (noun)   adjective

This dinner looks good.   pronoun   (verb)   adverb

Power is out to the whole block.   noun   verb   (adjective)

We will be there soon.   (adverb)   noun   verb

Day 7

Day 7: Adverbs and Adjectives	Language Arts 5

Choose the word that correctly finishes the sentence. Is the sentence missing an adverb, or an adjective?

My son was acting _____ last night.
suspicious   (suspiciously)

He seemed _____ but would not tell me why.
(excited)   excitedly

I _____ asked him about it again this morning.
curious   (curiously)

He simply smiled _____.
happy   (happily)

He _____ ran to his room.
eager   (eagerly)

In a few minutes he returned, trying to keep a _____ look on his face.
(serious)   seriously

He _____ pulled a wrapped gift from behind his back and yelled, "Happy birthday!"
quick   (quickly)

I love my _____ little guy.
(generous)   generously

Day 9

Day 9: Adverbs • Parts of Speech	Language Arts 5

Underline the word in each sentence that is an adverb.

We are going to arrive soon.

He can jump high!

They quietly entered the silent library.

The giant panda was walking backward.

We always drink water with our meals.

The goofy dog leaped enthusiastically.

The Christmas story is very beautiful.

Circle the part of speech that correctly labels the underlined word in each sentence.

Singing is somewhat enjoyable.   noun   (adverb)   pronoun

My daughter plays soccer.   verb   (noun)   adjective

The band was exceptional.   (verb)   pronoun   adverb

My favorite sweater has a hole.   noun   verb   (adjective)

Express yourself politely.   adverb   (pronoun)   verb

Day 13

Day 13: Writing	Language Arts 5

Write one tangible (physical, touchable) and one intangible (not tangible) thing that can answer these questions. If you can't think of answers to these, but you can think up your own questions and answers, feel free to use your own questions.

(Answers will vary)

What are big?
tangible: _____ the universe

intangible: _____ love

What are thieves?
tangible: _____ jaybirds

intangible: _____ worry

What's good medicine?
tangible: _____ a nap

intangible: _____ laughter

Think About It: If malice or envy were tangible and had a shape, it would be the shape of a boomerang.
-Charley Reese

Day 14

Day 14: Action/Imperative Verbs, Adverbs	Language Arts 5

Tell whether the underlined word is an action verb, an imperative verb, or an adverb by circling your choice.

"Hurry!" shouted my mother.   imperative

The dog licked the bowl greedily.   adverb

Are you jumping to conclusions?   action

It will start getting colder soon.   adverb

I think our rehearsal went well.   action

Write a poem using at least two similes. Can you make your poem rhyme?

_____

_____

(answers will vary – poem should include two comparisons using like or as.)

Day 17

Day 17: Sentence Quiz	Language Arts 5

Answer the following questions about sentences. Learn from any mistakes!

Which of the following is a complete sentence?
a. The talented photographer.
(b) He spends a lot of time perfecting his work.
c. Photographs of birds and nature.

What kind of sentence is this: Don't forget to empty the trash.
a. interrogative   b. declarative   (c) imperative   d. exclamatory

Use this sentence for the next 3 questions: The giant bulldog chased me down the street.
What is the simple subject of the sentence?
a. me   b. chased   c. the street   (d) bulldog

What is the simple predicate of the sentence?
a. giant   b. down   (c) chased   d. down the street

Which choice has a line drawn between the complete subject and the complete predicate?
a. The giant bulldog chased/me down the street.
b. The giant bulldog chased me down/the street.
c. The giant/bulldog chased me down the street.
(d) The giant bulldog/chased me down the street.

Which of the following is not a run-on sentence?
a. We traveled all over the country, we did it last summer.
b. We visited many places The Grand Canyon was my favorite.
c. My brother liked Carlsbad Caverns, my sister liked Niagara Falls.
(d) I had a great time, but nothing beats sleeping in your own bed.

Complete the writing assignment from your Lesson Guide.

_____

_____

_____

Day 18

Day 18: Noun Quiz	Language Arts 5

Answer the following questions about nouns. Learn from any mistakes!

Which list contains all of the nouns in this sentence?
The dog captivated the crowd with his loops and daring flips.
a. dog, crowd, daring, flips
b. dog, captivated, with, daring
(c) dog, crowd, loops, flips

Which sentence has all common and proper nouns written correctly?
(a) Last week Dad went to Metro Zoo with my brother.
b. They saw lots of Grizzly Bears, Panda Bears, and Polar Bears.
c. My Brother's favorite was the Churro Cart.

Which nouns correctly fill in the blanks of the sentence?
We picked lots of _____ from the _____ in the _____.
a. berrys... bushes... valleys
b. berries... bushes... vallies
(c) berries... bushes... valleys
d. berrys... bushes... valleys

Which nouns correctly fill in the blanks of the sentence?
While catching _____, the man used two _____ of cheese and some _____.
a. mouses... slices... potatoes
b. mice... slicies... potatos
c. mouse... slices... potatoes
(d) mice... slices... potatoes

Which answer has the same meaning as the words in bold?
The ball belonging to the girls went over the fence.
(a) The girls' ball
b. The girl's ball
c. The girls ball

Which answer has the same meaning as the words in bold?
The brother of James is named Andrew.
a. James' brother
(b) James's brother
c. James brother

Day 19

Day 19: Quiz • Metaphors • Spelling	Language Arts 5

Which sentence has a line between the complete subject and the complete predicate?
a. My brother and I went to the library yesterday.
(b) My brother and I/went to the library yesterday.

What is the simple predicate of this sentence?
My mother washed the purple dishes in the sink.
(a) washed
b. in
c. washed the purple dishes
d. in the sink

What is the subject of this sentence?
Please wash your hands and come to the table.
a. hands
b. your hands
c. table
(d) you

Which answer has the same meaning as the words in bold?
The uniforms of the officers were navy blue.
a. The officer's uniforms
(b) The officers' uniforms

Complete the following metaphors by filling in the blank. **(Answers will vary)**

His mind is a steel trap.   Laughter is good medicine.

Her room is a pigsty.   The moon is a disco ball.

Add an -ing to the following words by dropping an e or doubling a consonant to spell them correctly.

hop   hopping   hope   hoping

share   sharing   run   running

Day 20

Day 20: Metaphor or Simile • Writing — Language Arts 5

Is the given example a metaphor or a simile? Circle the correct answer.

She has a heart of gold.	(metaphor)	simile
Her hair shines like the sun.	metaphor	(simile)
The snow was a white blanket.	(metaphor)	simile
We were as snug as a bug in a rug.	metaphor	(simile)
My brother is a couch potato.	(metaphor)	simile
Her tears fell like raindrops.	metaphor	(simile)
He's as fast as a cheetah.	metaphor	(simile)
She is a pig at the dinner table.	(metaphor)	simile
They ran like a herd of elephants.	metaphor	(simile)
The storm roared like Godzilla.	metaphor	(simile)

Bonus tricky one:
My heart was a racehorse as I rode the rollercoaster.   (m)   s
("as" is not part of the comparison but is a word telling when)

Write a short poem using one metaphor.

_____

(answers will vary)

_____

_____

Day 29

Day 29: Spelling • Punctuation — Language Arts 5

Fill in the missing letter for the words below. Some are easy, some are hard!

bel i eve	tom o rrow	bas e ball
para c hute	independ e nce	calend a r
s q uirrel	def i nitely	ans w er
sep a rate	cou g h	k nife
suppose d ly	camo u flage	sc h ool

Did you know? The diacritic dot on top of the lowercase letters i and j is called a tittle.

Fill in the missing punctuation from the sentences below based on the hints given.

Fill in 2 semicolons:
Lincoln, Nebraska; Juneau, Alaska; and Helena, Montana are state capitals.

Fill in 2 commas:
"I'm not sure," I said, "that this the best route to the grocery store."

Fill in 2 commas:
July 4, 1776, was on a Thursday.

Fill in 1 semicolon and 2 commas:
I used to dislike tomatoes, green beans, and lettuce; now I'm enjoying their flavor.

Fill in 3 missing punctuation marks:
"What's your name?" I asked the small blond boy in the corner.

Day 31

Day 31: Metaphors • Commas — Language Arts 5

Answer the following questions about metaphors by filling in the bubble next to your choice.

What do metaphors do?
- ○ compare two unlike things using like or as
- ● compare two unlike things without using like or as

Is this a metaphor? Her heart was stone.
● yes   ○ no

Is this a metaphor? I'm as happy as a clam.
○ yes   ● no

Is this a metaphor? It's easy, like taking candy from a baby.
○ yes   ● no

Is this a metaphor? The mall is a zoo.
● yes   ○ no

Write in the commas where they belong in the following sentences.

Surprisingly, our team made it to the championship game this year.

As the underdogs, no one expected us to win.

Being a new team, it took us a while to find our groove.

To get us to bond as a team, our coach took us camping.

At the campground, we did many team building exercises.

After a while, we started winning games.

Completely unexpectedly, we took home the championship trophy.

Day 32

Day 32: Adjective Quiz — Language Arts 5

Answer the following questions about adjectives. Learn from any mistakes!

Which word in this sentence is an adjective?
The veterinarian gave a shot to the sickly dog.
a. veterinarian   b. gave   c. shot   (d.) sickly

Which bolded word is not an adjective?
a. We went to see the **travelling** circus.
b. My sister enjoyed the **goofy** clowns.
c. My **little** brother liked the elephants.
(d.) My **favorite** part was the acrobats and their flying.

Which of the choices is the correct form of the superlative for the sentence?
That was the _____ sunset I've ever seen.
a. colorful
b. colorfulest
(c.) most colorful
d. most colorfulest

Which choice correctly completes the sentence?
Your handwriting is _____ than mine.
a. best
b. more better
c. gooder
(d.) better

Which words correctly complete the sentence?
_____ ball over there is _____ interesting shade of blue.
(a.) That... an
b. This... an
c. Tho... a
d. Those... a

What is the correct way to write the proper adjective in the sentence?
The south african choir blessed us with their beautiful music.
a. South african
(b.) South African
c. south African
d. south african

Day 33

Day 33: Misused Words — Language Arts 5

The underlined words are incorrect. Write the correct word on the line.

Change the verb to match the plural subject.
The twelve birds <u>sings</u> a song.   **sing**

Change the subject pronoun to an object pronoun.
The teacher called <u>we</u> out for talking.   **us**

Change the verb to match the singular subject.
My dog <u>fetch</u> his ball when I throw it.   **fetches**

Change the object pronoun to a subject pronoun.
<u>Us</u> thoroughly enjoyed the movie.   **We**

Now it's your turn to find the incorrect word. Underline the incorrect word and write the correct word on the line. Can you fix the last two without a hint?

Find a plural verb that disagrees with a singular subject.
My friend Sam <u>ride</u> his bike every day.   **rides**

Find an object pronoun that should be a subject pronoun.
<u>Cade and me</u> went to the library together.   **I**

Correct the pronoun.
I'm going to teach <u>they</u> how to bake cookies.   **them**

Fix the subject/verb disagreement.
The three little kittens <u>loses</u> their mittens.   lose | **lost**

We'll all <u>goes</u> down to the park after our snack.   **go**

My sister <u>dress</u> her baby doll each morning.   **dresses**

Day 34

Day 34: Grammar Quiz — Language Arts 5

Answer the following questions about sentences. Learn from any mistakes!

What is the simple subject of this sentence?
The huge rainbow in the sky was a beautiful sight.
(a.) rainbow
b. sky
c. sight

What is the simple predicate of this sentence?
The children giggled loudly as they played in the yard.
a. children
(b.) giggled
c. played

Which words correctly complete this sentence?
I had _____ my arm on the monkey _____.
a. broke... bar's
b. broken... bar's
c. broke... bars
(d.) broken... bars

Which contraction correctly replaces the words in bold?
We **should have** known the traffic would be bad today.
(a.) should've
b. should'of
c. shoulda
d. should'av

Which bolded word is an action verb, not a linking verb?
a. It **seemed** dark outside.
(b.) I **looked** out the window to see why.
c. It **was** a rainy day.
d. Maybe tomorrow **will be** sunny.

Which word correctly completes this sentence?
Wet socks are the _____.
a. baddest
b. most bad
(c.) worst

Day 37

Day 37: Plurals • Writing — Language Arts 5

Which choice is the correct spelling of the plural of the word in parentheses?
(Volcano) are fascinating parts of nature.
(Volcanoes)   Volcanos   Volcanose

The (deer) were drinking from the meandering stream.
deers   (deer)   deeres

The (hero) saved the day for the trapped hikers.
heros   herose   (heroes)

The various choices of cake (mix) made her head spin.
(mixes)   mixs   mixies

The (bunch) of (cherry) were squished on the ground.
bunchs... cherrys   (bunches... cherries)   bunchs... cherries

Did you know? Some nouns can only be singular. *Information*, *wealth*, and *dust* are a few examples of **singulare tantum** (Latin for "singular only") nouns.

Write the three main points for your essay on the lines below.

1. _____

2. _____

3. _____

Day 38

Day 38: Correct the Sentences — Language Arts 5

Use the clues to help you rewrite the sentences correctly.
Find 2 punctuation and 2 word usage mistakes in each of these sentences.

"You is come to my house today" said Brandon.

"You **are coming** to my house today," said Brandon.

Thats mine mom over their by the water fountain.

That's **my** mom over **there** by the water fountain.

Find 3 misspelled words and 2 punctuation mistakes in these sentences:

The churchs on Spring Streat have steaples but the ones on Oak dont.

The **churches** on Spring Street have **steeples**, but the ones on Oak **don't**.

The potatos tomatos and peachs were all fresh.

The **potatoes, tomatoes, and peaches** were all fresh.

The underlined words are incorrect. Can you figure out why and fix them?

My neighbor <u>think</u> we are being <u>to noisey</u>?

My neighbor **thinks** we are being **too noisy**.

You're book is the most big Ive ever scene.

Your book is the **biggest I've ever seen.**

Day 39

Day 39: Pronouns — Language Arts 5

Which pronoun correctly fits in the blank for the sentence?

Jamie and _____ went to the mall yesterday.
(I)   me   myself

It was _____ who spilled the milk.
(I)   me   myself

Mom asked Alan and _____ to clean up.
I   (me)   myself

_____ share a closet since we wear the same size.
(My sister and I)   My sister and me   My sister and myself

Dad was unhappy with _____ drawing on the walls.
I   me   (my)

_____ report was the most interesting.
Naomi and yours   (Naomi's and your)   Naomi's and your's

_____ choosing where we eat will upset everyone.
(My)   Me   Myself

Between you and _____, I prefer the pink shoes.
I   (me)   myself

Our giggling gave away _____ hiding spot.
(Jenny's and my)   Jenny and my's   me and Jenny's

_____ are happy to share a pizza.
Jason and me   (Jason and I)   Jason and myself

Day 41

Day 41: Spelling
Language Arts 5

One of the underlined words in each sentence is misspelled. Can you correct it?

We all <u>tromped</u> down the <u>stairs</u> to <u>(brakfast)</u>

breakfast

A <u>(seargent)</u> a colonel, and a captain were all in uniform.

sergeant

My <u>chameleon</u> used his <u>(camoflage)</u> to hide from me.

camouflage

The dirty <u>(landrey)</u> pile was completely ginormous.

laundry

How many words can you make from the letters in the box below? Only use letters that are adjacent to each other (see the example).

C	L	A	S	E	L	A	R
M	I	S	H	E	F	L	Y
E	E	S	H	T	A	N	K	S
L	P	E	O	L	C	N	P
O	A	T	U	S	T	E	A
N	E	O	E	L	T	K	S
C	S	E	S	E	D	L	T
H	R	H	T	C	K	H	M
A	I	C	A	R	N	T	A

(answers will vary - possible words)

claims — shelf

melons — chairs

thanks — cheese

snake — shark

Day 42

Day 42: Subject and Object Pronouns
Language Arts 5

Fill in the missing pronouns with one of the choices. Does the sentence need an object pronoun or a subject pronoun?

Ezra, Briley, and I went to the store. __We__ bought cookies.
We / Us

Michael kicked the ball that fell right at __his__ feet.
his / him

Daniel and Nathaniel are friends. __They__ do a lot together.
Them / They

__We__ are happy to help. We won't complain.
We / Us

Is this invitation for __me__ or for you?
me / I

Brooke made herself a new skirt. It fit __her__ perfectly.
she / her

Peter, Samuel, and Andrew play chess and __they__ are good.
them / they

Chase and __I__ are the chess champions.
me / I

Braden and Bristol can juggle because I taught __them__
them / they

You should learn badminton from Iris and __me__.
me / I

Day 43

Day 43: Pronouns
Language Arts 5

Circle the pronoun that best fits the blank.

Try to do it by _____ next time.   myself (yourself) you

Matthew earned _____ own money.   him your (his)

Jessica and Kaitlyn called _____ mom.   (their) her his

Can _____ please feed the cat?   (you) us her

Ashlyn sang a solo by _____.   yourself (herself) her

The problem solved _____.   (itself) him me

Joshua is smart. _____ likes math.   Him His (He)

Karl and Jenn cleaned _____ home.   its (their) me

Alex wears glasses. _____ likes them.   Her (She) Hers

Eliana's dress is so bright _____ shines.   her (it) he

_____ will be late to the play.   (We) Them Her

John and _____ went to church.   my me (I)

_____ wanted to start a business.   Them Her (He)

Listen to Dad and _____.   my (me) I

Day 44

Day 44: Irregular Verb Quiz
Language Arts 5

Which irregular past tense verb best fills in the blank in the sentence? Learn from any mistakes!

The storm _____ to let up after its after deluge.
b. begun   (b.) began   c. beginned

I am _____ a lifelike rendition of Dr. Martin Luther King, Jr.
(a.) draw   b. drawed   c. drawn

My dad is good with tools and _____ us a backyard treehouse.
a. builded   b. build   (c.) built

A gentle breeze _____ on that fine, spring morning.
a. blown   (b.) blew   c. blowed

We _____ the candles on the cake and promptly set off the smoke alarm.
a. lighted   b. lited   (c.) lit

Isaac _____ the football so hard it left a mark on my hand.
(a.) threw   b. throwed   c. through

The area rug was full of dust and dog hair so we _____ it outside.
b. shaked   b. shaken   (c.) shook

We all _____ the shooting star as it streaked across the sky.
(a.) saw   b. seen   c. had saw

I _____ the entire week trying to build my new Lego set.
a. spended   (b.) spent   c. spend

Rebecca _____ her lunch to school every day.
a. bring   b. brang   (c.) brought

Sara _____ the balloon the most during the balloon toss.
a. catched   (b.) caught   c. cat

Our house _____ the third day on the market.
a. selled   b. saled   (c.) sold

Day 46

Day 46: Alphabetical Order • Sentences
Language Arts 5

Put these lists in alphabetical order. If the first letters match, move on to the second letter, and on down the line until you find a different letters.

January, February, March, April, May, June, July, August, September, October, November, December

April, August, December, February, January, July, June,

March, May, November, October, September

strawberry, bridge, grandmother, strap, bring, falcon, plentiful, fabulous, plantation, straw, football, giraffe

bridge, bring, fabulous, falcon, football, plantation,

plentiful, strap, straw, strawberry

Put a check mark if the sentence is complete. If it's not complete, make it a complete sentence using the lines provided.

All of the beautiful leaves of red, orange, and yellow×

(answers will vary, example:) crunched under my feet.

I am sad. ✓

The juicy burger satisfied my hunger. ✓

Christmas morning at the Rutherford household×

(answers will vary, example:) was a glorious, chaotic time.

Day 48

Day 48: Dialogue Punctuation • Writing
Language Arts 5

Do you remember how to properly punctuate dialogue? Fill in the bubble next to the sentence that is punctuated properly.

○ "I am ready to go home now." said Amanda.
○ "I am ready to go home now" said Amanda.
● "I am ready to go home now," said Amanda.

○ "Well," I replied, "I'm not quite ready to go."
● "Well," I replied, "I'm not quite ready to go."
○ "Well" I replied "I'm not quite ready to go."

● "Is there anything I can do to help you?" Amanda asked.
○ "Is there anything I can do to help you"? Amanda asked.
○ "Is there anything I can do to help you," Amanda asked?

● I answered, "Let me think."
○ I answered "Let me think."
○ I answered, "Let me think".

○ "Oh, I've got it," I exclaimed!
● "Oh, I've got it!" I exclaimed.
○ "Oh, I've got it." I exclaimed.

○ "You can find my keys," I suggested, "we need those to leave."
○ "You can find my keys", I suggested, "We need those to leave."
● "You can find my keys," I suggested. "We need those to leave."

● "They're in your hand!" she laughed.
○ "They're in your hand," she laughed!
○ "They're in your hand." She laughed.

Day 49

Day 49: Dialogue Punctuation • Writing
Language Arts 5

Correct these sentences. Add all missing punctuation and underline words that should be capitalized.

"<u>i</u> have two cats," <u>peggy</u> said. "<u>do</u> you have any pets?"

"<u>i</u> have two dogs," said <u>joe</u>, "as well as three fish and seven snails."

"<u>i</u> work at a pet store," said <u>jeremy</u>. "<u>does</u> that count?"

"<u>i'm</u> not sure," said <u>sue</u>, "if <u>i've</u> ever had a pet."

Write a dialogue between you and someone in your family OR anyone you like.

_____
_____
_____
_____
_____
_____
_____
_____

Day 51

Day 51: Parts of a Story
Language Arts 5

Answer these questions about the different elements of a story.

Which of these would be the **setting** of a fairytale?
(a.) a kingdom far, far away and long, long ago
b. a prince or princess

Which of these describes the **characters** in a story?
a. the moment of conflict in the story
(b.) who is involved in the story, both heroes and villains

Which of these might be the **plot** of a story?
a. Colonial America, 1600s
(b.) Against all odds, a group of dreamers breaks away from the rule of their country to start a new life in a new world.

Which of these describes the **conflict** of a story?
(a.) the problem the main character needs to solve
b. when two characters in the story fight each other

What happens in the **climax** of the story?
(a.) the conflict is resolved, often by a villain being defeated
b. the setting is revealed

What is the **resolution** of the story?
a. the characters make fresh goals as a result of the climax
(b.) we find out what happens to the characters after the conflict is resolved

---

Day 52

Day 52: Subject and Predicate
Language Arts 5

Underline the complete subject and circle the complete predicate.

<u>The hall closet</u> (houses the mop, broom, and vacuum)

<u>The never-ending movie</u> (rolled on and on)

<u>My mom and dad</u> (have been married twenty-five years)

<u>The bright red sock</u> (left balls of fuzz on the carpet)

<u>The three girls</u> (were very chatty)

<u>The lamp's light</u> (burned brightly in the otherwise dark room)

Write in the blank whether the underlined portion of the sentence is the complete subject (CS), complete predicate (CP), simple subject (SS), or simple predicate (SP).

The boy's many <u>chores</u> awaited.   CS

The television set <u>blared loudly</u>.   CP

Three dogs <u>chased</u> the ball down the road.   SP

The blustery wind blew the curtains to and fro.   SS

Her sympathetic look warmed my heart.   SS

I am so very hungry.   CS

The toddlers' giggles <u>were heard for miles</u>.   CP

Day 53

Day 53: Spelling • Writing
Language Arts 5

Fill in the lists below using the words in the box.

match	bread	laugh	tread	plump	botch
knot	guess	tough	sense	clan	clamp
love	fluff	bench	pinch	lick	plug

Short a spelled a
- match
- clan
- clamp

Short a spelled au
- laugh

Short e spelled e
- bench
- sense

Short e spelled ea
- bread
- tread

Short e spelled ue
- guess

Short i spelled i
- pinch
- lick

Short o spelled o
- botch
- knot

Short u spelled u
- fluff
- plump
- plug

Short u spelled ou
- tough

Short u spelled o
- love

Day 54

Day 54: Spelling • Writing
Language Arts 5

Use the words in the box to fill in the blanks below.

match	bread	laugh	tread	plump	botch
cough	guess	tough	sense	clan	clamp
love	fluff	bench	pinch	lick	plug

Write synonyms for the words below from the words in the box.

hard __tough__ giggle __laugh__ mess up __botch__

seat __bench__ thick __plump__ family group __clan__

Fill in the sentences with the word that best fits from the box.

We should replace our tires since they have no __tread__.

These socks don't __match__!

I have a big __knot__ in my shoelaces.

Can you __guess__ how old I am?

Your answer made no __sense__.

Don't __lick__ the spoon and put it back!

You forgot to __plug__ the tub and now the water is gone.

My cat is just a big ball of __fluff__.

In a __pinch__ I can substitute oil for butter.

Day 56

Day 56: Spelling
Language Arts 5

Fill in the lists below using the words in the box.

claim	play	crave	cloak	meet	leap
slow	seam	kind	hide	splice	boot
yolk	creed	blow	laid	pray	haste

Long a spelled a-e
- crave
- haste

Long a spelled ai
- claim
- laid

Long a spelled ay
- play
- pray

Long e spelled ee
- creed
- meet

Long e spelled ea
- seam
- leap

Long i spelled i
- kind

Long i spelled i-e
- splice
- hide

Long o spelled o
- yolk

Long o spelled oa
- cloak
- boat

Long o spelled ow
- slow
- blow

Day 57

Day 57: Spelling
Language Arts 5

Use the words in the box to fill in the blanks below.

claim	play	crave	cloak	meet	leap
slow	seam	kind	hide	splice	boot
yolk	creed	blow	laid	pray	haste

Write synonyms for the words below

nice __kind__ tunic __cloak__ not fast __slow__

jump __leap__ ship __boat__ quickness __haste__

Write the word in the blank that best replaces the underlined words.

I have a strong desire to eat pizza. ___crave___

The sewn edge of my shirt sleeve is splitting. ___seam___

The middle of my egg is still runny. ___yolk___

I talk to God first thing each morning. ___pray___

We went to see the theater production. ___play___

I affirm that he is my dad. ___claim___

I set down the baby in his crib. ___laid___

Put out of sight that chocolate cake. ___hide___

Can we come together at the mall? ___meet___

Day 58

Day 58: Compound and Complex Sentences
Language Arts 5

Write whether the sentence is compound or complex on the line beside the sentence.

Some days are easy, and some days are hard. ___compound___

If you want to come over, I can serve dinner. ___complex___

When the phone rang loudly, it made me jump. ___complex___

My dad had the steak, but I had the fish. ___compound___

Add a clause from the box to complete each sentence. Write the letter of your choice and then whether the resulting sentence is compound or complex.

a. If your bike tires are flat	d. and I need to go to the post office
b. but she couldn't	e. when you come inside
c. Should we start eating	f. Before you sign

I need to go to the bank, __d__. ___compound___

__c__, or should we wait for everyone? ___compound___

__a__, pump them up with air. ___complex___

__f__, be sure to read the entire document. ___complex___

She tried to enjoy the movie, __b__. ___compound___

Please wipe your feet on the mat __e__. ___complex___

Write one compound sentence and two complex sentences on the lines.

_____

_____

_____

Day 59

Day 59: Writing Voice
Language Arts 5

Different styles of writing will lend themselves to different writing voices. Match the example sentence to the type of writing it represents.

    a. compare/contrast   c. persuasive argument

    b. personal narrative   d. humorous description

I believe homeschooling should be legal worldwide. ___c.___

I was thrilled to hear we were arriving at the park. ___b.___

Snails are small, but ladybugs are much smaller. ___a.___

Her hair spilled willy-nilly over her shoulder like pasta. ___d.___

Match the underlined portion of the paragraph with the "voice problem" it represents.

    a. slang   b. too formal   c. too informal

1. Our vacation was totally rad. 2. We went to Laguna Beach, California (as if you needed to know the exact location). 3. I and my basic unit of society had a really nice time together.

1. __a.__   2. __c.__   3. __b.__

Add descriptive words and phrases to the sentences below, but keep them all in the same voice - don't mix formal and informal choices, don't be silly in one and factual in another. When you are finished, read through the whole paragraph out loud and see if it sounds consistent throughout. (answers will vary, example only)

Yesterday was a great day. The weather was __delightful__! I went outside and __basked in the glow of the sunshine__ as I __frolicked through the yard, completely carefree__. I could hear the __gentle rustling of the leaves as the breeze blew__. Indeed, it was a marvelous day.

Day 60

Day 60: Word Choice
Language Arts 5

Which word choice strategy do the underlined words represent?

    a. strong verb   c. vivid adjective

    b. sense image   d. exact noun

1. The pine was swaying in the breeze. 2. It towered above the other trees as it covered and uncovered the sun, 3. making dancing shadows on the ground. 4. Its majestic limbs gently swung to and fro.

1. __d.__ 2. __a.__ 3. __b.__ 4 __c.__

Which of the options given is the more vivid word choice?

The river (meandered/went) through the woods. ___meandered___

The soccer team was (hungry/famished). ___famished___

Let's go to (a restaurant/Big Mama's Deli) for lunch. ___Big Mama's Deli___

The snake (moved/slithered) along the path. ___slithered___

Replace the underlined word in each sentence with a more vivid word. (answers will vary)

I had fun at the fair. _____

My brother is a funny guy. _____

The ride home was long. _____

We went to the store for snacks. _____

She is my best friend. _____

I thought dinner was good last night. _____

Write a complex sentence.

_____ (answers will vary)

_____

Day 61

Day 61: Spelling • Writing Rubric
Language Arts 5

Fill in the lists below using the words in the box.

fuse	lunar	loot	pew	cruise	feud
loom	accuse	fruit	mood	view	hooks
tooth	cook	books	flume	refuse	lose

The u sound found in booth spelled:

oo
- loom
- tooth
- loot
- mood

u-e
- flume

u
- lunar

o-e
- lose

ui
- fruit

ui (cruise)
- cruise

The u sound found in few spelled:

u-e
- fuse
- accuse
- refuse

ew
- pew
- view

eu
- feud

The oo sound in crook:

cook   books   hooks

Day 62

Day 62: Spelling
Language Arts 5

Use the words in the box to fill in the blanks below.

fuse	lunar	loot	pew	cruise	feud
loom	accuse	fruit	mood	view	hooks
tooth	cook	books	flume	refuse	lose

Write synonyms for the words below.

molar __tooth__ bake __cook__ fight __feud__

treasure __loot__ deny __refuse__ sight __view__

Fill in the sentences with the word that best fits.

I think we might have blown a __fuse__.

Don't bother him; he's in a bad __mood__.

You should be a good sport, even when you __lose__.

Did you see the __lunar__ eclipse?

Make sure you eat enough __fruit__.

Did you __accuse__ me of lying?

The coats were all hanging on the __hooks__ in the closet.

We sat down on the hard __pew__.

That's a large stack of __books__!

Day 64

Day 64: Complete Sentences

Write C if the words make a complete sentence. Write F is the words make a sentence fragment. Write RO if the words make a run-on sentence.

It's summer!	C
Time to go to the pool.	F
I love to float on my back in the water.	C
Sunscreen, towels, sunglasses, and dive sticks.	F
I like the sun. I like the water.	RO

Correct the run-on sentences by writing and, but, or or on the line and adding a comma where you would add them to make a compound sentence.

I want to play, I am sick today.	but
Do you like pizza, do you prefer hot dogs?	or
I like vacation, there's no place like home.	but
My favorite color is blue, I also like red.	but/and
We could watch a movie, we could play a game.	or/and

Turn these sentence fragments into complete sentences on the lines.

Early on Saturday morning.

(answers will vary)

The pile of dirty laundry.

Running and jumping.

The book on the table.

Day 65

Day 65: Possessive Nouns

On the first line, write whether the noun is singular (S) or plural (P). On the second line, make the noun possessive.

foxes	P	foxes'	Riley	S	Riley's
children	P	children's	houses	P	houses'
book	S	book's	men	P	men's
money	S	money's	deer	S/P	deer's
papers	P	papers'	cherries	P	cherries'

Change the underlined words into possessive nouns by either writing in an apostrophe or an apostrophe s.

The dolphins' tails were slapping the water.

We went to the children's museum last week.

Monday's power over people's moods is pretty strong.

The women's restroom had a long line.

The Kellers' home was bustling with people.

We really enjoyed Nashville's downtown scene.

The flood damaged all of the books' spines.

Change the underlined words into possessive nouns.

The theories of scientists don't always agree.	scientists' theories
We played with the cards belonging to Emily.	Emily's cards
The hula hoops used by the girls were pink.	girls' hula hoops
Don't forget to bring the sunscreen you own.	your sunscreen
The songs of the children rang out beautifully.	children's songs

Day 66

Day 66: Spelling • Possessive Nouns

Fill in the lists below using the words in the box.

march	stare	flair	chart
stair	heart	mare	bear
market	scarce	pardon	

The ar sound found in far spelled:
ar

march	market
chart	ear
pardon	heart

The air sound found in chair spelled:
are air

stare	stair
mare	flair

ar-e ear

scarce	bear

Write a possessive noun into the blanks in the sentences. (answers will vary)

My _____ computer is on the fritz.

The _____ giggles filled the air.

A bunch of _____ heads appeared in the water.

We had a great time at _____ birthday party.

Your _____ water bowl is empty.

Day 67

Day 67: Spelling • Writing

Use the words in the box to fill in the blanks below.

march	stare	flair	chart
stair	heart	mare	bear
market	scarce	pardon	

Write synonyms for the words below.

step __stair__   horse __mare__   store __market__

few __scarce__   gaze __stare__   pizazz __flair__

Fill in the sentences with the word that best fits.

Exercise is good for your __heart__.

Show me the graph from your __chart__.

This burden is too much to __bear__.

Please __pardon__ me, for I need to leave early.

The band likes to __march__ in formation.

Write a short description of your favorite place in nature. See if you can use possessive nouns to make your writing better.

Day 68

Day 68: Adverbs

Each of these sentences has too many adverbs. Choose one adverb and cross the others out so the sentence is more readable. (Answers will vary. Of the underlined choices, all should be crossed out but one in each sentence.)

Our big family frequently runs out of milk often.

They boisterously ran around the room loudly.

We occasionally usually go to the park normally.

The girls were overly, amazingly, extremely excited it was Christmas.

Please quickly come here immediately!

We will soon be going shortly.

She quietly whispered to her sister softly.

Write your own adverb in the blank, using the words in parentheses to guide you as to what type of adverb to use. (Answers will vary. Here are suggestions.)

The class sat __impatiently__ as they waited for the teacher. (how)

I left my book __there__ by the table. (where)

We __always__ go to church on Sundays. (when)

Sheila recites multiplication facts __impressively__. (how)

I __thoroughly__ enjoy the symphony. (how)

I'm sure it's __somewhere__, we just need to look. (where)

__Tomorrow__, we will go to the zoo. (when)

Day 69

Day 69: Commas

Which of the choices have the commas in the right places? Fill in the bubble next to your answer.

- ● We can play the game, but we need to clean our room first.
- ○ We can play the game but we need to clean our room first.
- ○ We can play, the game, but we need to clean our room first.

- ○ Understandably she was upset at the news, that her dog had died.
- ● Understandably, she was upset at the news that her dog had died.
- ○ Understandably, she was upset at the news, that her dog had died.

- ● We are going to San Antonio, Texas, after Thanksgiving.
- ○ We are going to San Antonio, Texas, after Thanksgiving.
- ● We are going to San Antonio, Texas after Thanksgiving.

- ● The purple, green, and blue flowers made a lovely bouquet.
- ○ The purple green and blue flowers made a lovely bouquet.
- ○ The purple green and blue, flowers made a lovely bouquet.

- ○ After a long day at the park we were ready for some water.
- ● After a long day at the park, we were ready for some water.
- ○ After a long day, at the park, we were ready for some water.

- ● The twins were born on Friday, October 27, 2006.
- ○ The twins were born on Friday October 27, 2006.
- ○ The twins were born on Friday, October 27 2006.

- ○ We can't find the hammer, but, we can find the wrench.
- ● We can't find the hammer, but we can find the wrench.
- ○ We can't find, the hammer, but we can find, the wrench.

- ○ If I don't have your number how can I call you?
- ○ If, I don't have your number how can I call you?
- ● If I don't have your number, how can I call you?

- ○ Dusty our 80 pound dog, still thinks he's a tiny puppy.
- ● Dusty, our 80 pound dog, still thinks he's a tiny puppy.
- ○ Dusty our 80 pound dog still thinks he's a tiny puppy.

Day 71

Day 71: Spelling

Fill in the lists below using the words in the box.

firm	smear	swerve	turf	blur	church
leery	learn	cheer	career	rear	germ
fear	squirrel	adverse	first	fern	gurgle

ur sound in turkey spelled:

ir
firm	
squirrel	
first	

er
swerve	
adverse	
fern	

ur
turf	
blur	
church	
gurgle	

er
germ

ear
learn

ear sound in dear spelled

ear
fear
smear
rear

eer
leery
cheer
career

Day 72

Day 72: Pronouns

Choose the correct pronoun for the sentence from the options given.

I would rather go with you than with _____ and _____.
- ● him and her
- ○ he and she

Each one of the cars had _____ windshield broken in the hailstorm.
- ○ their
- ● its

_____ runners like to have a certain kind of shoe.
- ● We
- ○ Us

Sometimes, motorists don't seem to care much about _____ runners.
- ○ we
- ● us

_____ and _____ don't always see eye to eye.
- ● She and I
- ○ Her and me

The football team went to _____ bus.
- ○ their
- ● its

The water droplets left _____ mark on the shower curtain.
- ● their
- ○ its

We were planning to split the work between Jamie and _____. In the end, I did it all.
- ○ myself... myself
- ● me... myself

Day 74

Day 74: Verbs

Replace the underlined words with a word from the box by rewriting the paragraph on the lines. Put the words from the box into the correct tense to fit the paragraph. When you're writing, try to use descriptive words such as the ones in the box to make your writing more exciting and descriptive.

ecstatic	adored	exhausted	excite	terrify

I love babysitting. I know it scares some people, but not me. Spending time with young kids is fun for me. I do come home at the end of a babysitting experience tired from all of my work, but it's worth it. I'm happy to think that one day I might be a parent and get to spend a lot of time with kids.

I adore babysitting. I know it terrifies some people,

but not me. Spending time with young kids is

exciting for me. I do come home at the end of a

babysitting experience exhausted from all of my work,

but it's worth it. I'm ecstatic to think that one day

I might be a parent and get to spend a lot of time

with kids.

Day 79

Day 79: Comparatives and Superlatives

Fill in the blank with the comparative or superlative form of the adjective in parentheses. Use the sentence for clues as to which one it's looking for.

It's **more peaceful** in my home at night than it is during the day.
(peaceful)

My absolute **worst** subject is math.
(bad)

I'm **better** at science than history.
(good)

Her hit went the **farthest** of all.
(far)

The fire truck's siren is **louder** than our car's horn.
(loud)

The **hottest** month of the year at my house is August.
(hot)

Your ice cream cone is **bigger** than mine.
(big)

The sky is **more colorful** than it was last night.
(colorful)

This is the **reddest** rose I've ever seen!
(red)

My mom is **shorter** than my sister.
(short)

This is the **happiest** he's been in a long time.
(happy)

Day 80

Day 80: Word Builder • Verbs

How many words can you make from the letters in the box below? Only use letters that are adjacent to each other (see the example).

C	L	A	L	A	C	R	A
M	I	N	T	P	O	S	M
R	S	E	A	E	R	A	T
A	R	K	O	H	K	E	Y
I	A	N	H	S	L	R	O
N	D	O	S	I	E	L	H
S	T	K	I	W	D	N	G
H	R	H	P	L	I	U	N
O	I	P	U	L	L	E	T

(Answers will vary. Suggestions below.)

claims	sharks
wiser	rake
maker	perks
weld	shirt

Identify the verb type that is underlined.

We <u>can't</u> go to the movies.
main verb   helping verb   (contraction)

We <u>are</u> going to dinner.
main verb   (helping verb)   contraction

Next week we'll <u>try</u> a movie.
(main verb)   helping verb   contraction

I <u>have</u> a theater coupon.
(main verb)   helping verb   contraction

Day 81

Day 81: Homophones • Word Search

Choose the correct homophone to fill in the blank of the sentence.

_____ going home.   Is that _____ book?
Their   (They're)   There   (your)   you're

Go _____ the tunnel.   My laces are in a _____.
(through)   threw   not   (knot)

The trailer on the truck will _____ the _____ to the farm.
hail... hay   haul... hey   hail... hay   (haul)   hay

Find the words below in the word search. Words are hidden in all directions.

artistic   neighbor
awkward   ravage
balcony   supposed
civilization   vanish
download   website

Day 84

Day 84: Possessive Nouns

Choose the correct sentence of each group of choices.

● The game's design was superb.
○ The games' design was superb.
○ The games's design was superb.

○ The shows' credits ran on and on.
● The show's credits ran on and on.
○ The showes credits ran on and on.

○ The childrens' game was over quickly.
○ The childrens's game was over quickly.
● The children's game was over quickly.

○ Its always nice when it's sunny outside.
○ It's always nice when its sunny outside.
● It's always nice when it's sunny outside.

○ The two city's streets intersected at the county line.
○ The two citie's streets intersected at the county line.
● The two cities' streets intersected at the county line.

● I've experienced three white Christmases.
○ I've experienced three white Christmas's.
○ I've experienced three white Christmas'.

○ Fridays' menu includes soup and sandwiches.
○ Fridays's menu includes soup and sandwiches.
● Friday's menu includes soup and sandwiches.

● Dr. Jennings' office called. Dr. Jennings is running late.
○ Dr. Jenning's office called. Dr. Jennings is running late.
○ Dr. Jennings's office called. Dr. Jennings is running late.

Day 86

Day 86: Unscramble • Conjunctions

Unscramble the following words taken from the book *Alice in Wonderland*. You can use the definitions given to help you figure out the word if you are stuck.

CMOK   mock
not authentic or real, but without the intention to deceive

XACO   coax
to try to persuade someone

TDAIRCCNTO   contradict
to make an opposite statement

OREVKOP   provoke
to anger, enrage, exasperate

UEEVNRT   venture
a risky or daring journey or undertaking

Choose the correct conjunction to connect the two parts of the sentence.

We can't go **until** you put your shoes on.
so that   until   as if

Do your work now **so that** you don't have to later.
so that   until   as if

You look **as if** you aren't feeling very well.
so that   until   as if

Day 94

Day 94: Capitalization

Choose the sentence in each group that is capitalized correctly.

● Mr. Mackey played the piano marvelously.
○ The giant pink Rabbit on the front of the card was creepy.
○ We had a Surprise Party for Ellie on Saturday.

○ The Atlantic ocean is smaller than the Pacific.
○ The Smartphone was so expensive.
● We need to head east on Lake Street.

○ My dad's favorite show is *The Cosby Show*.
● My mom prefers to read *Where the Red Fern Grows*.
○ My sister wrote a play called *West Of The Mississippi*.

○ Our favorite destination is rome, Italy.
○ George Washington was the first President of the United States.
● I read an interesting article about Mickey Mantle.

○ "Let's go," Mom called, "for we're almost late."
○ "I'm not sure," Sally said, "What your point is."
● William shouted, "come back with my ball!"

Answer whether each part of this letter uses proper punctuation.

Dear Sir or Madam:
● yes   ○ no

Enclosed please find a refund for your endowment check to the metro zoo; our bee exhibit just didn't fly.
○ yes   ● no (Metro Zoo should be capitalized as a proper noun)

Sincerely,
John Hanson
● yes   ○ no

Day 96

Day 96: Capitalization • Irregular Plurals

Choose the sentence in each group that is capitalized correctly.

● Let's go to South Carolina for our history trip.
○ The Psychology Test was really hard.
○ The Football team was on a hot streak.

● We went to Paris on our last vacation.
○ Charlotte is in north Carolina.
○ My Insomnia is acting up tonight.

○ The seattle Space Needle is a tourist attraction.
● We drove to Disneyland last Saturday.
○ His sport coat was a slick shade of Gray.

● "Can you please come here?" my mother asked.
○ Is friday the last day of this month?
○ My favorite player is Ken Griffey jr.

○ My geography project was on south America.
○ The Strawberry Milkshake was so creamy.
● We saw *The Tempest* on stage last year.

Make the words plural on the lines beside them.

mosquito	mosquitoes	mouse	mice
wolf	wolves	tray	trays
goose	geese	cactus	cacti
crisis	crises	ox	oxen

Day 97

Day 97: Irregular Plurals • Commas

Correctly write the plural of the word on the line.

person	people	tooth	teeth
calf	calves	bush	bushes
radius	radii	oasis	oases
index	indices	loaf	loaves
child	children	sheep	sheep

Did you know? The correct plural of *octopus* is *octopuses*. *Octopi* became the assumed plural when Latin plurals were added to words, until scholars pointed out that *octopus* comes from the Greek. That makes *octopuses* the correct plural.

If a comma belongs in the box, fill it in. If no punctuation belongs in the box, leave it blank.

If you want good home cooking☐ for a great price☐ you should go to☐ Mama's Little Bakery☐ the best eatery in town.

Leaving for the wedding a little late☐ we weren't sure if we would☐ make it on time☐ but we hit all the lights and got there☐ right as the service was starting.

We were so excited for our aunt☐ to come visit☐ that we forgot to☐ finish our school work☐ for the day.

Day 98

Day 98: Irregular Past Tense

Choose the correct past tense verb to fit the sentence.

The wind **blew** all of the leaves into the street.
blowed   blown   blew

We **brought** our dog to the vet.
brought   bringed   brang

We have all **seen** this movie already.
saw   seen   seed

Your dog **bit** my finger taking the ball.
bited   bit   bitten

Mr. Hinkle **took** my dad's parking spot.
took   toked   taken

We **spent** the entire day at the park.
spended   spending   spent

Pizza with pepperoni **became** my favorite meal.
becomed   became   become

She **fell** and skinned her knee.
fell   falled   fallen

Day 99

Day 99: Irregular Past Tense
Language Arts 5

Choose the correct past tense verb to fill the sentence.

She __held__ my hand tightly during the storm.
holded   held   hold

Mr. Gilman __knew__ the whole song by heart.
knowed   known   knew

Are you the one who __stole__ my bike?
stole   stealed   stolen

The president __spoke__ at our local high school.
speaked   spoken   spoke

He has __written__ a brilliant essay on slavery.
writed   wrote   written

The sun __rose__ over the hill.
rose   rised   risen

Her phone __rang__ so loudly it startled me.
ringed   rung   rang

We've __ridden__ our bikes up that steep hillside.
ridden   rided   rode

Day 100

Day 100: Apostrophes
Language Arts 5

Fill in the missing apostrophes from the sentences below. Remember that apostrophes show possession like Mary's book or the three girls' dresses.

Mr. Driscoll's cat hopped up onto our fence.

Jamie's car was a cherry red color.

The Randalls' house was at the end of its street.

The four boys' shoes were muddy from the rain.

Sam's dog chased Tamara's rabbit across the street.

Patrice's purse's strap was caught in the car's door.

My two marbles went down the track's hill.

The fireworks' pops were loud to Tiffany's ears.

Will you grab Sue's books and yours off the shelves?

The worksheet's questions were full of tricks.

The bowl's design made it perfect for chips.

Day 101

Day 101: Unscramble • Writing
Language Arts 5

Unscramble the following words taken from the book Little Men. You can use the definitions to help you figure out the word if you are stuck.

ESNIUTINA   __insinuate__
suggest or hint (something negative) in an indirect and unpleasant way (i, a)

QITAUCA   __aquatic__
of or relating to water (a, c)

OOPCCIEURS   __precocious__
having developed certain abilities or proclivities at an earlier age than usual (o, s)

ETMNUCEBR   __recumbent__
lying down (c, t)

DNIETEMRT   __detriment__
a cause of harm or damage (d, t)

UVLACTTEI   __cultivate__
try to acquire or develop (a quality, sentiment, or skill) (c, e)

MEAEGEINR   __menagerie__
a collection of wild animals kept in captivity for exhibition (n, e)

ELAABIM   __amiable__
having or displaying a friendly and pleasant manner (a, e)

Day 102

Day 102: Proofreading
Language Arts 5

Correct the mistakes in the sentences below. Underline the words that need to be capitalized, cross out capital letters that should be lowercase or punctuation that shouldn't be there, and add in any missing punctuation. Some sentences have clues, but others you'll need to read carefully to make sure you don't miss anything!

Find 5 capitalization mistakes and 3 punctuation mistakes in each of these sentences:

my favorite authors are lewis, tolkien, and gunn.

my friend sara's favorite movie is disney's aladdin.

"You're a hard worker," My Mom said as i swept the floor.

Find 5 total mistakes in each of these sentences:

I like Winter and I like Summer, too.

my Aunt does all of her shopping on amazon.

cara was born on thursday, march 4, 2010.

You're on your own with these! Find the mistakes and correct them.

"Don't touch the hot stove!" Said dad.

the Blue Stick was dried up when the girls tried to use it.

Last year, chelle's family went to utah to ski.

Day 103

Day 103: Proofreading • Writing
Language Arts 5

The underlined words are not correct. Write the correct word on the line.

The four girls shares a room.   __share__

The children read its books.   __their__

The teacher taught he class.   __his__

Her went to the library weekly.   __She__

Can I come to you house today?   __your__

Now you find the incorrect word in the sentence. Underline it and write the correct word on the line.

Not many people has seen that movie.   __have__

Many people is excited for Christmas.   __are__

Follow ours directions to the park.   __our__

She loves check the mail every day.   __checking__

Would your like to ride bikes?   __you__

The cat ate all of their food.   __its__

Can you come with Sandra and I?   __me__

Write a sentence that is a list of things containing subjects and predicates.

__(answers will vary)__

Day 104

Day 104: Proofreading
Language Arts 5

Fix the underlined part of each sentence by writing the correct sentence on the line.

what is your favorite thyme of year. mine is fall

__What is your favorite time of year? Mine is fall.__

Mr. doyle played Soccer with the kids in mexico?

__Mr. Doyle played soccer with the kids in Mexico.__

I wrote a Thank You card to nurse Linda for her care.

__I wrote a thank you card to Nurse Linda for her care.__

Now find the mistakes yourself. Write the correct sentences on the line.

doughnuts cakes and candies are nice in moderation?

__Doughnuts, cakes, and candies are nice in moderation.__

On are way to cedar point we had a flat tire.

__On our way to Cedar Point, we had a flat tire.__

You're book was left, on the mantle, at grandmas.

__Your book was left on the mantle at Grandma's.__

Day 106

Day 106: Spelling
Language Arts 5

The underlined words are spelled incorrectly. Can you spell them correctly on the line?

The dore needs to be shut. It's cold outsied!

__door__   __outside__

We culd go on the rode and ride our bikes.

__could__   __road__

The blew sweater is so warm and fussy.

__blue__   __fuzzy__

Now find the mistakes yourself. Write any incorrectly spelled words on the line.

Tomorow is Independance Day in Amurica.

__Tomorrow__   __Independence__   __America__

The dog's tale was waging feuriously at the site of the cat.

__tail__   __wagging__   __furiously__   __sight__

Can you poor me a dreenk? My glass is emptie.

__pour__   __drink__   __empty__

Day 107

Day 107: Prepositions
Language Arts 5

Remember that a preposition is always part of a prepositional phrase. Tell whether the underlined word is being used as a preposition or not by circling your answer.

The kids swam across the pool.   (yes)   no

The dog ran through the flower bed.   (yes)   no

Put the remote down!   yes   (no)

The bird soared over the trees.   (yes)   no

She loves to dress up her dolls.   yes   (no)

Quit horsing around and get to work!   yes   (no)

Underline the prepositional phrases in the sentences below.

Put the book on the table.

Come and warm up beside the fireplace.

You have what it takes within you!

Put the plant beside the window to give it more sunlight.

Day 108

Day 108: Prepositions • Writing
Language Arts 5

Read this story. It is full of prepositions. Can you underline each one?

My dog's name is Dusty. He's a busy dog. He loves to run around the coffee table. He likes to sit on the hearth of the fireplace. Sometimes he hides under the blankets of my bed.

He enjoys playing in the yard. When I accidentally throw his ball outside the fence, he tries to jump over the fence to retrieve it! Once he chose to do that rather than go through the open gate.

Dusty can be mischievous. He once buried my mom's gardening gloves beneath the maple tree in our yard. Yet he is the sweetest dog I know. When I'm scratching him under his ears and he's snuggled in my lap, all is right with the world.

Write a few sentences about an imaginative game that you have played.

__(answers will vary)__

Day 109

In the following sentences, put a line under the subject and put a line over the predicate (highlighted for clarity). Then circle the prepositional phrase and draw an arrow pointing to the prepositions. The first one is done for you.

Kinley and William gave their books to the librarian.

Would you like to have bacon with your eggs?

My father should be home around dinnertime.

Please grab the cereal from the pantry. (subject is implied)

Iris put all of the DVDs on the shelf.

Chase piloted the plane above the clouds.

The boys played hockey until dark.

I love my brother's new bike. (no prepositional phrase)

Can you help me with the dishes?

Audrey hit the softball over the fence.

The girls ran all the way home from rehearsal.

Write a few sentences about a time that you apologized to someone for spoiling their fun and tried to make them happy again.

_____

_____

_____

_____

Day 112

Tell whether the underlined word is a preposition or the object of the preposition.

Andrew did his math worksheet at the table.
(preposition)   object of the preposition

Sandra and Jane rode their bikes to the park.
preposition   (object of the preposition)

Across the river, we found a neat trail.
preposition   (object of the preposition)

The cat was hiding inside the litter box.
(preposition)   object of the preposition

Can you fit everything in your suitcase?
preposition   (object of the preposition)

What time is it on the clock on the stove?
(preposition)   object of the preposition

The object of the preposition is marked. Underline the preposition.

What time is it on the clock on the stove?

Beneath the surface of the earth, molten lava flows daily.

Hiking the snowy peaks of Mt. Everest is on my bucket list.

Have you heard the news about the Mexican earthquake?

There was a thunderstorm during the night.

Day 113

Underline the preposition in the following sentences. Remember that a preposition has to be part of a prepositional phrase.

We enjoy swimming during the summer.

Don't try to walk across the busy street.

My dog chased a squirrel up a tree.

I would love to travel around the world.

I like playing dress up with my little brother.

We spun around on the merry-go-round.

Answer the following questions about prepositions.

Which of these words cannot be used as a preposition?
○ above   ○ between   ● worse   ○ with

Which sentence has the preposition in bold?
○ I'd love to go with you to the concert.
○ My favorite group will be singing.
● We can ride together in the same car.
○ We can sing songs all the way home.

Which sentence has the prepositional phrase in bold?
○ I took my cousin to the park.
● He liked going up and down on the see saw.
○ He also enjoyed the slide because it was really fast.
○ It was hard to get him to come home.

Day 115

Fill in each blank with the correct word. Each blank will either need they're (a contraction meaning they are), their (shows ownership), or there (a place).

We really enjoyed watching __their__ soccer game.

What's that bright light over __there__ ?

__Their__ mom said they need to come home.

__They're__ all tired from a long day at the lake.

__They're__ putting __their__ books over __there__ .

See how many words you can come up with using the grid of letters below. Only use letters that are adjacent to one another as you have done in the past. This grid is smaller than the last one, can you still do it? (Answers will vary.)

E	R	A	T
F	M	L	S
O	E	R	U
D	I	C	E

framer	dice	mode
salt	tale	male
dome	rats	rice

Day 116

Underline the prepositional phrases in the following sentences.

After the news, my favorite show comes on.

I keep all of my money in my piggy bank.

I went into the bedroom to get my book.

The eagle soared over the lake with elegance.

Let's go around the corner and see Grandma.

The woodpecker hit his beak against the tree.

I put my pulled tooth under my pillow.

Please get in the car so we can leave.

Big fireworks exploded above our heads.

The boat drifted on the open sea.

Our wheels spun rapidly as we flew down the road.

The rainy skies put a damper on our town parade.

The ponies trotted around in a circle.

Could we go to the park today?

Day 117

Using your same sentences from day 116, now underline the preposition and circle the object of the preposition. Remember that both of those will be contained within the prepositional phrase.

After the news, my favorite show comes on.

I keep all of my money in my piggy bank.

I went into the bedroom to get my book.

The eagle soared over the lake with elegance.

Let's go around the corner and see Grandma.

The woodpecker hit his beak against the tree.

I put my pulled tooth under my pillow.

Please get in the car so we can leave.

Big fireworks exploded above our heads.

The boat drifted on the open sea.

Our wheels spun rapidly as we flew down the road.

The rainy skies put a damper on our town parade.

The ponies trotted around in a circle.

Could we go to the park today?

Day 118

Fill in the correct pronoun to be the object of the preposition. If you're having trouble figuring it out, read the sentence out loud with both choices. Whichever one sounds right is probably the right answer.

Can you put a blanket over __him__ ?   him   he

Let's go with __them__ to the store.   them   they

Alyssa read a book to __her__ .   she   her

The bugs were swarming around __us__ .   we   us

Huge birds circled in the sky above __me__ .   me   I

Behind __him__ I saw a huge skunk.   him   he

Will you bring the phone to __me__ ?   I   me

You can just go around __them__ .   they   them

She got what was coming to __her__ .   her   she

You are welcome to come with __us__ .   us   we

The blanket is under __him__ so it's stuck.   he   him

She wants you to come to __her__ .   she   her

Day 119

Answer the following questions about sentences. Learn from any mistakes!

What is the preposition and object of the preposition in this sentence? The group of friends all had ice cream in little paper cups.
a. the/friends
b. all/friends
c. had/ice cream
d. in/cups

What is the complete prepositional phrase in this sentence? The enormous rainbow could be seen over the rooftops all morning.
a. The enormous rainbow
b. could be seen
c. over the rooftops
d. all morning

Which bolded word is not used as a preposition?
a. Katie rode her bike down the street.
b. She turned to go around the corner.
c. As she turned, she fell off the bike.
d. That turned her smile upside down.

Which of the answers given is an adverb in this sentence? My best friend goes to church here with me.
a. goes
b. to
c. here
d. with

Which sentence uses the correct form of the adverb to fill in the blanks? This cake is so ___; she bakes really ___.
a. good/well
b. good/good
c. well/good
d. well/wall

Which words correctly fill in the blanks of this sentence? We don't have ___ more crackers, and there ___ no peanut butter, either.
a. no/is
b. any/is
c. any/isn't
d. no/isn't

Day 121

Choose the sentence of each group that is written correctly.

○ Those boys shouts are hurting my ears.
○ Those boy's shouts are hurting my ears.
● Those boys' shouts are hurting my ears.

● The other children's artwork is more colorful than mine.
○ The other childrens' artwork is more colorful than mine.
○ The other childrens artwork is more colorful than mine.

○ The horse had it's hooves cleaned by the stable boy.
● The horse had its hooves cleaned by the stable boy.
○ The horse had its' hooves cleaned by the stable boy.

○ Why is the womens' room line always longer than the mens'?
○ Why is the womens room line always longer than the mens?
● Why is the women's room line always longer than the men's?

○ All the area church's services were canceled by the hurricane.
● All the area churches' services were canceled by the hurricane.
○ All the area churches services were canceled by the hurricane.

○ Drew's and Gracie's mom was PTA president.
● Drew and Gracie's mom was PTA president.
○ Drew's and Gracie mom was PTA president.

Now you fill in the missing apostrophe(s) for the sentences below.

The people's appointments were late when the doctor got a flat tire.

The cherry's stem was the ornament's hook.

Day 122

Day 122: Grammar Review
Language Arts 5

Of the bolded words, circle the one that matches the part of speech to the side of the sentence.

We all went to the (busy) restaurant last night. — Adjective

I'm too busy to do it (myself). — Pronoun

The (busily) buzzing bee pollenated the flower. — Adverb

I want to go for a (run) later tonight. — Noun

Can you (think) about what you want for dinner? — Verb

I listened to a loud storm (during) the night. — Preposition

(Yesterday) was the Christmas parade in town. — Adverb

Today (was) a very long day. — Verb

Have you been (to) the bank yet today? — Preposition

The (swirly) bubbles floated through the air. — Adjective

His (courage) was obvious. — Noun

Will (you) please bring me the remote? — Pronoun

Day 124

Day 124: Prepositions • Parts of Speech
Language Arts 5

Color in the bubble next to the list of prepositions in each group.

- ● down, beside, behind
- ○ fling, sprint, devour
- ○ tall, red, calm
- ○ quickly, yesterday, soon

- ○ truly, madly, deeply
- ○ run, jump, fly
- ● up, to, with
- ○ rosy, happy, fragrant

- ○ beautiful, fabulous, lazy
- ● aboard, within, toward
- ○ always, only, usually
- ○ maple, novel, school

Did you know? There are 8 main parts of speech: nouns, pronouns, verbs, adjectives, adverbs, prepositions, conjunctions, and interjections. How many have you learned?

Write the part of speech of the bolded word in the blank.

I only have time for one more game. — adverb

Would you like to **come** with me? — verb

Do you have the desire **within** you? — preposition

That is such a **lovely** dress. — adjective

The elegant **deer** leapt into the woods. — noun

Are you able to do it **yourself**? — pronoun

Day 126

Day 126: Loose or Lose
Language Arts 5

Choose the correct word to fill in the blank. By the end of the worksheet you should be certain which word has which meaning.

You'd better hurry up so you don't _____ your place in line.
○ loose ● lose

The whole dresser collapsed because of one _____ screw.
● loose ○ lose

Her _____ tooth made it hard to eat.
● loose ○ lose

Did you _____ any teeth yet this year?
○ loose ● lose

I counted all of my _____ change and can afford a drink.
● loose ○ lose

_____ the dog from the leash so he can run.
● loose ○ lose

The slower runner will _____ the 50-yard dash.
○ loose ● lose

I hope you never _____ your love of learning.
○ loose ● lose

The _____ board on the deck is a tripping hazard.
● loose ○ lose

Day 127

Day 127: Word Search
Language Arts 5

Use the definitions to find the words from the book Little Men in the word search puzzle. Words can be any direction.

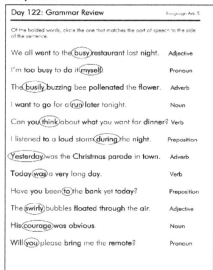

- indignant
- irreplaceable
- ingratitude
- impressible
- magnanimous
- perversity
- salable
- vaguely

Day 128

Day 128: Grammar Review
Language Arts 5

Of the bolded words, circle the one that matches the part of speech to the side of the sentence.

The kids went canoeing on the (choppy) lake. — Adjective

Please come with (us) to our delicious dinner. — Pronoun

The elephants (loudly) trumpeted their trunks. — Adverb

The blue umbrella shielded us from the (rain). — Noun

The sweet sisters (held) hands as they skipped. — Verb

We ran (down) the lane as we sang the song. — Preposition

Write the part of speech of the bolded word in the blank.

I **pinched** my finger in the sliding door. — verb

My sister's **sickly** eyes were red. — adjective

The **lightning** flashed brightly in the sky. — noun

A gigantic river flowed **to** the sea. — preposition

The **painfully** aching tooth throbbed. — adverb

The massive fan blew **our** hair all over. — pronoun

Day 129

Day 129: Summarize
Language Arts 5

Read each short paragraph. Then choose the sentence that does the best job summarizing the paragraph. For the last one, write your own summary sentence.

Genevieve was having a great kindergarten year. She had learned the alphabet and how to read small words. She had learned to count as high as one hundred. She knew lots of colors and shapes.
- a. Genevieve knew the alphabet.
- b. Genevieve could count high.
- (c.) Genevieve was learning a lot in kindergarten.
- d. Genevieve liked school.

If you have trouble with responsibilities, a virtual pet may be for you. You still have to feed it and clean up after it, but there are no real-life consequences if you forget or get lazy with it. Learn some responsibility with a virtual pet!
- a. Virtual pets save puppies.
- b. It doesn't hurt a virtual pet if you forget about it.
- c. A virtual pet is cleaner than a regular pet.
- (d.) Virtual pets are a safe way to learn responsibility.

Justin inhaled the cold air through his nostrils and smiled. He was giddy as the snow crunched under his feet. In his mind, nothing was better than exploring fresh snow and then warming up with hot chocolate. Winter was great!

(answers will vary)   Example: Justin liked winter.

Day 130

Day 130: Whose or Who's
Language Arts 5

Choose the correct word to fill in the blank. By the end of the worksheet you should be certain which word has which meaning.

Do you know _____ sweater this is?
● whose ○ who's

I'm the only one _____ home sick today.
○ whose ● who's

_____ afraid of spiders?
○ Whose ● Who's

Gretta is a girl _____ hair is as bright as the sun.
● whose ○ who's

That boy is Tommy, _____ father is in the army.
● whose ○ who's

André is a boy _____ tough to beat in soccer.
○ whose ● who's

I wonder _____ coming to the Christmas party.
○ whose ● who's

_____ sponsor is Adidas?
● Whose ○ Who's

_____ being sponsored by Nike?
○ Whose ● Who's

Day 137

Day 137: Writing – Plot
Language Arts 5

Make a list of at least three plot events. What's the character going to do first? Then what's going to happen? What are some things that the character could learn along the way? List a few ideas.

(answers will vary)

Write the number of the idiom beside its meaning.

1. Bring home the bacon — 7 — be really excited about something
2. Hit the nail on the head — 4 — make someone mad
3. Deer in the headlights — 1 — make money for your family
4. Drive someone up the wall — 8 — be in a bad situation
5. Have your ducks in a row — 3 — be startled by something
6. Hit the hay — 5 — be organized
7. Be on cloud nine — 6 — go to bed
8. Be in a pickle — 2 — get something exactly right

Day 141

Day 141: Proofreading
Language Arts 5

Answer the questions about the following paragraph. Use the numbers to help direct you to the right part of the paragraph.

1. Lightning is a fascinating phenomenon. 2. A single bolt of lightning is 54,000 degrees Fahrenheit. 3. A single bolt of lightning is about five times hotter than the surface of the sun. 4. Around the world, lightening strikes more than three million times a day. 5. That's about forty times per second. 6. It also kills around too thousand people a year. 7. Always respect the power of lightning!

Which of these is the best way to combine sentences 2 and 3?
- ○ A single bolt of lightning is 54,000 degrees Fahrenheit which makes a single bolt of lightning about five times hotter than the surface of the sun.
- ○ A single bolt of lightning is 54,000 degrees Fahrenheit and a single bolt of lightning is about five times hotter than the surface of the sun.
- ● A single bolt of lightning is 54,000 degrees Fahrenheit, or about five times hotter than the surface of the sun.

What change should be made to sentence 4?
- ○ Remove the comma
- ● Change lightening to lightning
- ○ No change

What change should be made to sentence 5?
- ○ Change that's to thats
- ○ Change second to secont
- ● No change

What change should be made to sentence 6?
- ○ Change the period to a question mark
- ● Change too to two
- ○ No change

We hope you had a great year with EP Language Arts 5.

EP provides free, complete, high quality online homeschool curriculum for children around the world. Find more of our courses and resources on our site, allinonehomeschool.com.

If you prefer offline materials, consider Genesis Curriculum which takes a book of the Bible and turns it into daily lessons in science, social studies, and language arts for your children to learn all together. The curriculum also includes learning Biblical languages. Genesis Curriculum offers Rainbow Readers and A Mind for Math, a math curriculum designed for about first through fourth grade to be done all together. Each math lesson is based on the day's Bible reading from the main curriculum. GC Steps is an offline preschool and kindergarten program. Learn more about our curriculum on our site, GenesisCurriculum.com.

Made in the USA
Columbia, SC
09 August 2019